THE

FIVE

PRINCIPLES OF GLOBAL TEAMS

LEADING ACROSS BOUNDARIES

Jay Clark, Ph.D.

ISBN 979-8-88851-692-8 (Paperback)
ISBN 979-8-88851-693-5 (Digital)

Covenant Books
11661 Hwy 707
Murrells Inlet, SC 29576
www.covenantbooks.com

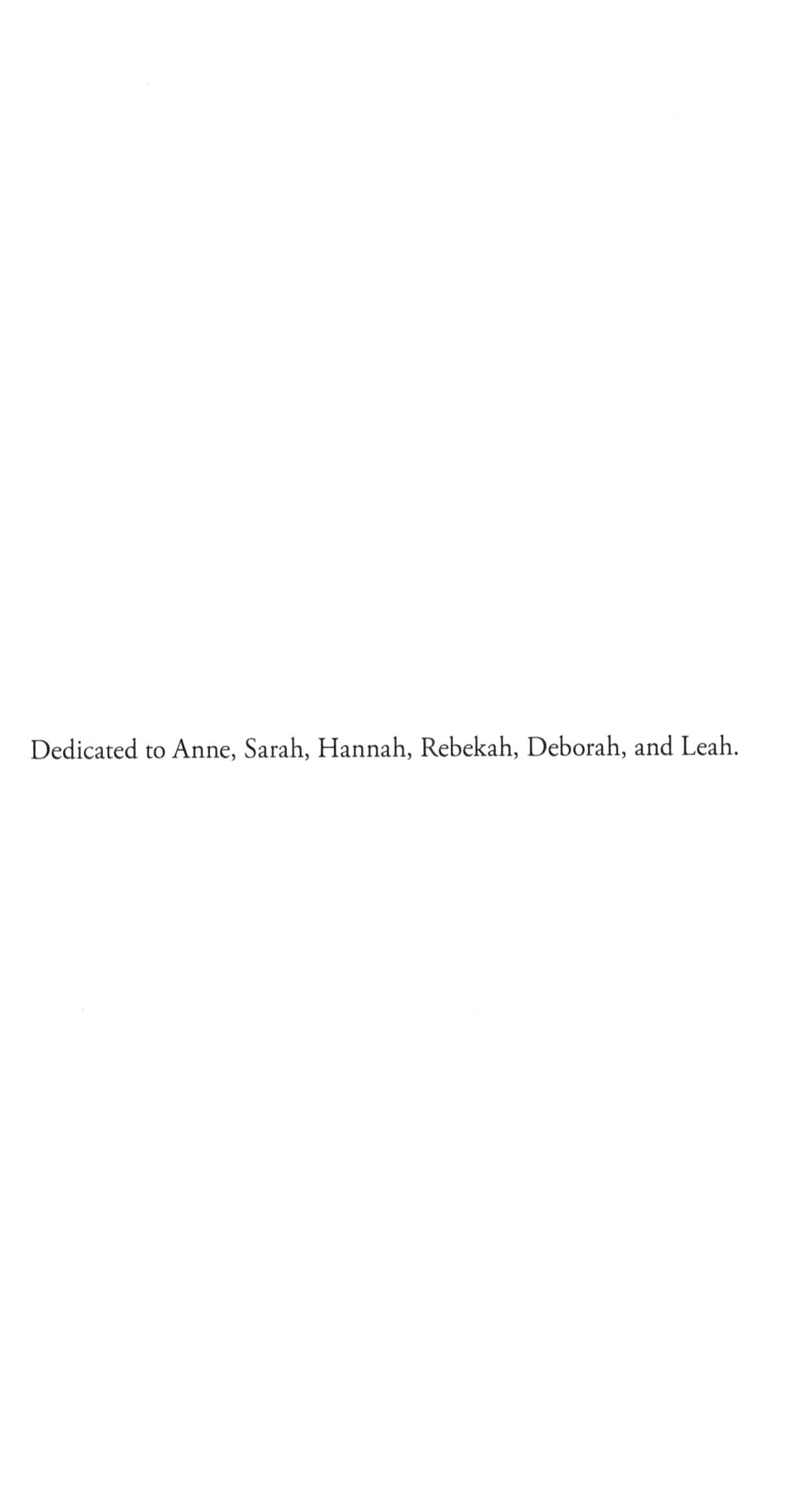

Dedicated to Anne, Sarah, Hannah, Rebekah, Deborah, and Leah.

Contents

Part 1

INTRODUCTION

The process of team building and teamwork has been an interest of mine for most of my life, beginning with an emphasis on sports in my youth. Whether it was baseball or American football, the team was the focus. I enjoyed the dynamics of being a team. The sad part was playing ten years in youth sports and being on more losing than winning teams. Constant issues with team sports led me to think a little deeper about the team process.

As I moved into my college years, the American culture started rearing the individualistic worldview, and I spent most of those years focusing on myself. These years significantly impacted me, and I kept that same mindset when I transitioned to my professional years. As I started my entrepreneurial career in the early 2000s, I began with this individualistic mindset. I believed I was alone, and my success depended on my ability.

For many years, I thought that was the correct path until I met the leadership challenges of 2008. The challenge was a mixture of personal health issues and the global economic crisis in Asia. While living in Hong Kong, my feelings of isolation felt intense, and the main problem was my individualistic mindset had only connected me to others with the same tendencies. At the time, I needed a strong team, and I only had working groups.

Going through 2008–2009 taught me the importance of teams. I started learning more about the difference in having teammates that shared the same vision, which brought about a shared burden to the risk and outcomes. I learned more about celebrating wins and enjoying the team's success. This outlook changed how I led my businesses, social groups, and family.

Over the last ten years, the research and practice were focused primarily on teamwork in a traditional/physical location. From these experiences, I have been passionate about teaching team building and leadership in MBA programs, consulting with organizations worldwide, and researching and writing about teams. Some of my favorite authors were Katzenbach and Smith with *The Wisdom of Teams* and Hackman's *Leading Teams*.

Because of the immediate need for virtual teams, many organizations have yet to learn how to build, design, and lead teams in this format. The problem is that the process of team building and leading teams has changed. The concept of virtual teams was starting to receive attention in research and writing, but with the onset of a global pandemic, the process has grown much faster.

In my book *The Five Principles of Global Leadership*, I described five principles that help leaders manage the complexities of global leadership. For this book, the process is similar in that I am not prescribing a method but instead using the same five principles to serve global leaders as they develop into influential global team builders. To help with the description, I will also use analogies such as networks to help global organizations design, build, and lead global teams. This process has always been complex, but it almost seems impossible in today's global environment.

Chapter 1

THE NEED

Why is it important to start by describing the need? As I write this book, we are coming out of a global pandemic and going into a global recession that is only causing more challenges toward global operations. Some researchers are calling it the "end of the global era" that started in the 1980s because of the rise of nationalistic agendas from politicians around the world. We are seeing protectionism happen worldwide in the USA, China, India, and other leading economies, but there is an unanswered question: Can we return to a place where global operations do not exist or are limited? I personally don't see this happening, but storms are brewing in large waves for global leaders, which is why this book is written for those global leaders with the future in mind and for those who need to expand to international operations. Don't worry, the end isn't near, but it will take global leaders with clear principles to succeed in the challenging times ahead and an organization's ability to create high-performing teams as a large part of enduring the future challenges.

I want to help global leaders create high-performing teams in the current environment. The current environment is not only about what COVID restrictions have caused us to adapt to but also about what the future holds with a connected world. We found out that technology allows us to work from anywhere and are moving away from gathering in one building; instead, we found employees can operate teams in many ways.

Now that we are moving past the pandemic, more assessment on virtual teams and how to measure if they are successful is underway. Can we use the same process of measuring success as the traditional approach? Research on team building shows that leading successful teams requires the following conditions: real teams, clear direction, enabling structure, supportive organizational context, and expert coaching. I will use similar terms in my book, but the process will be different as a network.

To help guide the process of creating, designing, and implementing successful global teams, I use the term network to help global leaders understand the process. It is easy to say we are connected like a digital network. Because of the global pandemic, we had to transform into a network that requires a digital feed to connect us. We were inside a secure firewall but not sitting together. In the future, global leaders must learn how to make the network stay *high speed* because no one likes to see buffering in the system. The book explores ways to keep the global team at a high-speed level and remove buffering to reach peak performance.

Future Organizational Challenges

With future challenges such as rapid technological changes, workforce adaptability, and the desire for more freedom, virtual teams will be around for a while; if anything, virtual teams will only increase. With higher speeds of the internet, we have become accustomed to technology such as Zoom and Microsoft Teams; the meetings do not feel as virtual as before, but even with this process, the mind knows you are far away from each other. Developers are trying to solve this problem by creating technology—adding another world between virtual and physical: augmented reality. It is a way to trick the mind into thinking you are physically together.

The progression of the virtual concept adds a layer of complexity for global organizations that have seen dramatically increased challenges over the last 20 years. The world saw an attack by a small group of terrorists on the world superpower on 9/11, and we witnessed and experienced the crushing defeats of a global recession in 2008–2009. We've seen governments partner and then break up (Brexit), and for the last few years, we've been devastated by a global pandemic. Despite all these challenges, there has been a constant search for a solution to sustain growth.

From the experience of trying to find solutions for organizations during these events, the best solution is building teams that can endure complexity and chaos while also finding ways to thrive during the process. These teams will allow organizations to grow and be a beacon for other groups to strive to match their performance. The risks are too high globally to place all assets in one place. Organizations must find ways to create, design, and build teams without the ability to structure the team in one location.

Many have solutions that combine the growth of technology and the ability to work together as a team. A team can no longer depend on physically being together or in the same time zone. Instead, the team will be fluid and diverse. The question is, What makes this environment conducive to a high-performing team? We are not describing a small group, but it's the unit team responsible for leading the organization through the challenges we've faced over the last 20 years. The teams create and implement strategy while initiating and leading projects. If the normal process of team building is removed, how do teams need to adapt to be successful?

In this type of environment, what is an effective high-performing team? In 2002, Hackman said that effective teams have high productivity and exceed the expectations of the team's clients. The increased productivity could be internal or external clients. To make it a real team, Hackman says you need a clear understanding of the team's work, who is on the team, the extent of the team's authority, and stable membership. For a globally networked team, we could still use the same type of measurement for measuring performance, but the process of how we team up is what is changing.

The networked global team is the best way to describe the type of team needed to succeed in this environment. For this reason, describing the teamwork process with the current and future challenges for organizations, especially with the increased complexities in the global environment, is becoming harder and harder.

Chapter 2

WHAT IS A GLOBAL TEAM, AND HOW DO THE FIVE PRINCIPLES HELP WITH PERFORMANCE?

The progression of complexity for global organizations has only increased dramatically over the last 20 years. Global leaders search for solutions to give the ability of an organization to not only sustain itself during these crises but find ways to grow. We have come to realize there will never be a "back to normal."

From the experience of trying to find solutions for organizations during these events, my consultations have a recurring theme. The best solution is building teams that can endure complexity and chaos while finding ways to thrive. These teams will not only allow organizations to grow, but they will be a beacon for other groups to strive to match their performance.

Organizations have tried various solutions to create effective teams. They often combine the growth of a different type of technology and try to piece those processes into the ability to work as a team. Many of these changes come from a team where no one can see each other face-to-face or is even dependent on being in the same time zone. This type of team is responsible for leading the organization through the challenges we've faced over the last 20 years.

The challenge for organizational leaders is how these processes can build a team's success culture. Suppose the traditional team approach of face-to-face meetings is no longer needed even when the teammates live in the same city or region, can a successful team culture be created to navigate the many challenges in the global environment?

There is a need to create a foundation for teams that assist them in whatever form they operate. I call them the core areas. The core areas for teams to develop a culture of success are shared vision, communication ability, and accountability. Using the concepts of these core areas, I found the right words to describe how organizations can effectively design, build, and lead successful teams with the increased complexities in the global environment. The best way to describe the type of team needed to succeed in this environment is the globally networked team.

When we think of the word *network*, we think of IT or a computer network that provides Wi-Fi to our devices. This type of connectivity is the reason I chose this word because that is the visualization needed to learn how a networked team operates. A network team must be connected but is not dependent on being physically together. A networked team must also be flexible and be on the move like you would, jumping from one Wi-Fi hotspot to another to stay connected in different environments.

With the analogy of the Wi-Fi network, there are many ways to describe how a network operates. The first important piece is that you must have a power source to run the network. Another critical part of the network is the equipment. With the growth of wireless technology, the network has expanded because you no longer must sit next to a plug for connectivity and electricity. My children have no idea what it was like during my childhood. The only way to receive a phone call was to sit next to the phone, and a cord connected to it, so I could only go very far with missing a call. In today's complex global environment, struggling organizations are still sitting next to the landline, worried they will miss the call.

The Three Core Areas of a Global Team

The networked team needs all members to have a certain mentality that motivates them to higher success. The mindset that works for networked teams is based on three core areas. They are a shared vision, communication, and accountability. As with the changing times, these terms mean differently from what they did with a traditional team having weekly in-person meetings. They are concepts you understand but have a twist to help navigate the challenges of the networked team.

Shared Vision

In any network, there is a requirement for a connection. This connection can come through satellites or lines of cable connecting continents. The how of networking is not the primary issue, but it is why the network is connected that is the primary concern. A shared vision is a mesh that makes the networked global team operate. It is the core of the existence of the team and the reason the team exists. It is only possible to lead a team with a shared vision because it would no longer be a team but a working group or committee.

In leading a networked team, there must be a strong shared vision. When a football team is on the pitch, it is easy to see the shared vision of the desire to win the match, but when the networked global team operates, the only proof of a shared concept is the outcomes. Leaders not only create a vision but also attract people who share the same vision. When people meet in person, a leader can sometimes use coercive or authoritative power to propel the team. The use of coercive power is rarely an option for networked teams.

There is a collaborative effort that only some try to reach when meeting in person. For this reason, a networked team needs leaders who share the same vision. They empower each other to lead when the team needs their strength in leadership.

In *The Five Principles of Global Leadership*, I called this shared vision part of the principles of strategy and sacrifice. It's easy to see the strategic aspect of having a shared vision, but what about the sacrifice aspect? When we use the word *sacrifice*, we're talking about giving up something. What does giving up part of your life to achieve a shared vision mean? Because of differences in culture, language, and social background, the networked team must learn to sacrifice to understand each other to create a shared vision that will inspire the entire team wherever they are located.

What type of sacrifice is necessary for the global team to become a network team? The first type of sacrifice is giving up specific identities to mesh into the network. Sacrificing identity is difficult because I am not saying you are no longer who you are. Still, instead, it is about a sacrifice that understands who you are but will make changes necessary to build strong relationships with your teammates. From my experience of leading teams around the world, most of the time, leaders coming from less developed areas of the world or willing to give up these sacrifices are much more manageable than leaders from the developed world.

Identity. One of the biggest challenges global leaders face in a networked team today is the concept of identity. We identify with our local environment more than the people across the world from us. We are experiencing massive refugee challenges stemming from countries' physical boundaries. As the vaccine for COVID-19 became available, we saw from the distribution the challenge of nationalism and the limits set up from that concept. The vaccine distribution was about who could pay the most to secure the doses needed for their country.

How does one identify in a networked team that crosses boundaries and national lines?

Whether physical, emotional, or cultural boundaries seem to pull us toward our local community, at times, it looks like global leaders are always swimming against the stream. Global leaders are challenged to influence people, so they will step out of their local environment and thrust them into an atmosphere of unknowns, differences, and obstacles. Why would leaders want to treat their followers that way? Why would leaders want to cross boundaries?

The issue of identity is about the debate on the ability to prove the differences between global and domestic leadership. Why is global leadership an issue? There are three reasons: the need, challenges, and opportunities for global leaders. It is not difficult to understand the need for global leaders who can make the world a better place. The challenge for global leaders is the complexity of leading across cultures. The opportunity is billions of people looking for influential global leaders to serve their villages, communities, countries, and regions.

The global leader is tasked with being able to serve where they are physically while also inspiring and motivating followers in other regions. The global leader must see locally and globally. It is like a person wearing bifocal eyeglasses. The lower part of the glasses allows the global leader to visit locally, and the higher side allows a global view.

How do the five principles help with performance?

To explain this process, we first need to review the five principles of global leadership. There are three concepts to explain: first, what a global leader is, the second is what a principle is, and the third is what the five principles are and why they are essential to global teams.

A global leader is a person who leads across cultures with systems, processes, and relationships in a complex environment.

Complex, cross-cultural leadership can happen within the geographic boundaries of one nation or can span over oceans and across multiple countries. I met with the organization's top leaders during my recent trip to India. I noticed that the leaders segmented and formed groups discussing issues in their mother tongues. Among the fifteen participants in the training, there were five different languages, five different people groups, and five different cultures. Therefore, English is the organizational language for most Indian companies. Even though the organization only operates inside the geographic boundaries of India, these leaders are global leaders.

Using the above definition, academic research, and my experiences, I will describe the five leadership principles that allow global leaders to manage the complexities of systems, processes, and relationships. These are the foundational principles that all leaders need to exhibit and are the building blocks for other necessary characteristics of an effective leader. We all have an opportunity to lead in some part of life. Still, those who implement principles of integrity, purpose, sacrifice, discipline, and compassion are most likely remembered as leaders who positively impact their organizations, communities, and the world. Suppose a person applies these characteristics to life; in that case, they will see fruit from the investment and build credibility and experiences that will attract followers. This process is essential because you are not a leader unless you have followers.

How do the five principles connect with a global team?

Principle	Description	Increases team performance
Integrity	Provides honest feedback in an appropriate and helpful manner, admits mistakes, doesn't misrepresent self for personal gain, maintains confidentiality, is seen as a truthful and trustworthy leader *Cognitive complexity* Moral choice, move past self-interested choices.	When a global leader adds servanthood with the integrity, there is an ability to manage and not abuse power and control. By focusing on the people, the global leader is serving first, then the organization increases effectiveness, which is why it is the first principle listed. *Key concepts for global teams* A. Collaboration B. Trust
Purpose	Understands and clearly articulates an inspired vision of the company's goals and mission, aligns team's goals with company's goals, committed to the company's core values and culture. *Cognitive complexity* Openness to learning from failure while developing strategy from a vision full of uncertainties.	When leading across cultures, the global leader must carefully communicate the vision to ensure it is effective in reaching the target audience. Articulating a vision depends not just on the words used but also on the leader's character and integrity. *Key concepts for global teams* A. Strategic B. Implementor

Sacrifice	Greater challenge for a global leader is sacrificing one's local identity to gain global followers. *Cognitive complexity* Using tension and conflict to spur new opportunities and reframe existing mindsets.	Global leaders are not unique in the sacrifice they have to make in order to be successful, but it seems at times that the sacrifice is greater when dealing with conflict and chaos in the team. Therefore, the global leader has to understand their identity in order to become effective as a global leader. They have to see beyond their fears to meet the challenges for the team, even if it means personal failure. *Key concepts for global teams* A. Belonging B. Engagement
Discipline	The ability to lead change also takes a discipline that is unique. *Cognitive complexity* Identify the need for change, create a change initiative and ability to implement the change initiative.	Discipline is an aspect of self-control. Being able to structure priorities for different teams around the world to know when and how to lead change takes a unique global mindset. A global leader must take time to make sense of the world. There is a challenge for the global leader to stay disciplined while adapting to the fast-paced global environment. The ability to lead change is unique. The self-control to manage pain and remedies to make change a success is the ultimate test of discipline. *Key concepts for global teams* A. Diagnosis B. Prescribing solutions

Compassion	Compassion is a hard trait to exhibit in one's own culture and even more so in multiple cultures. How a global leader communicates with and treats the next generation of leaders is as important as the process.	To meet these complexities, the principle of compassion helps the team leader start a transformation process to lead the culture of the team. The process of compassion then leads to the advantage of the team in the rate of success in learning and multiplication.
	Cognitive complexity	
	Building nonlinear and unpredictable relationships.	*Key concepts for global teams* A. Self-learning B. Multiplication

With a *glocal* (global and local) vision that sacrifices one's own identity for the sake of others is how we explain a shared vision. This shared vision can be great, but it is only limited if the team can communicate it through the network. Therefore, communication is critical to the networked team.

Communication

For a network to work, it must send a signal, either wired or wireless, so that the equipment can be functional. A network does not operate if it is not connected to the internet. In the same way, a networked team cannot operate without communication. If shared vision is the mesh of the networked global team, then communication is the signal that connects the network.

Communicating in a networked team is different; you cannot send hand signals or use body language to communicate. It requires the ability to write clearly and speak concisely. An essential part of this communication is understanding that the network has specific protocols to be followed for communication to be effective. If it doesn't have the correct IP address, it doesn't go to the right computer or smartphone; instead, the team must understand that communication must be thorough and precise. An effective networked team cannot depend only on one form of communication, such as text or email; it must be a clear communication strategy that includes boundaries.

How a networked team communicates is one that poses many risks of misunderstanding. For a team to build a network of communication, it requires two different types of understanding. The first is understanding how to communicate; the second is the execution of communication. When a team is centrally located, communication can be more accessible because you get to know each other's forms of expression. Using body language, a teammate can determine if someone is in a good or bad mood or engaged. All these cues and signs are much harder to determine over text and video chat.

For this reason, a networked team must have an ability to execute communication. To accomplish the communication execution of a networked team is to model the three Ts. They are timing, tool, and tone. The three Ts illustrate the need for a leader to be concise and understand that communication is not just about a directive but also about influence and empowerment.

When a global leader decides to communicate part of the shared vision, they must understand the importance of timing. Of course, you must think, *If the person awake right now, what is the last thing they read before they go to bed or the first thing they read when they wake up in the morning?* A teammate needs to understand how they handle certain situations in the morning than in the evening.

Along with making sense of the actual time of receiving the information, the global leader shows emotional intelligence with the timing. The team's importance is supporting each other like a network that supports each other to get the job done. The team leaders understand their team's emotional circumstances to understand the timing of the communication.

A networked team is more thought out than you would if you regularly meet each other at a physical office space. You can't just ask a teammate in a networked team to meet for a coffee or go to lunch. Therefore, a team must create a process for strategic communication. Once you make sense of the situation and understand that your teammates' emotional state is essential, you decide on the tool.

Strategic communication

Strategic communication is called a direction-giver. An effective direction-giver breaks down communication into the skills of a doer, follower, and guide. These actions are practical and needed in the networked team since they do not focus on one leader to provide communication. All the members will need to know how to use these skills strategically to succeed as a networked team.

Strategic communication shows the importance of ethics, morals, and values in direction-giving. Because group dynamics are changing, direction-givers must respond appropriately when others in the group communicate their needs and act appropriately to attract attention and trust. During these actions, a doer, follower, and guide must exercise skillsets in promoting credentials, demonstrating competence, and building credibility.

Ultimately, strategic communication is about a person's ability to persuade others. By the influence of values and character on direction givers skillsets such as doers, followers, and guides, a person can determine that an effective follower makes an effective leader. For a networked team, the doer, follower, and guide have three distinct traits in their character that are important for their strategic communication. They are their intentions, good sense, and good moral character.

1. *Intention.* When a networked team is communicating strategically, there is always a need to clarify the intentions. The communication shows there are good intentions behind the request. Motivation and manipulation are a fine line. The team cannot feel they are being manipulated into a decision.

2. *Good sense.* Later in the book, we will discuss the importance of sensemaking in adapting, but this type of good sense is different. It is more about being clear and concise. Strategic communication cannot be vague and general. The networked team needs to be able to refer to the com-

munication for "marching orders," which is the to-do list for the shared vision.

3. *Good moral character.* The networked team's success depends on more than just a few words on a poster or whiteboard. The success of the team is based on action. We are living out the process of good intentions, good sense, and moral character. The actions of leaders are where trust is created and sustained. Words help us describe our actions, but be clear that actions are first and primary.

Good sense and moral character need clear guidelines, and a networked team allows monitoring of those guidelines. Monitoring is unlike a *Big Brother* watching the process as a lord over the system. The process is monitored through a compassionate heart that seeks not to blame but to develop to make the team better through accountability.

Accountability

A shared vision is the network mesh, and communication is the network's signal. Accountability is the firewall of the network team. A firewall is there to stop unauthorized access into the network to keep it from viruses which will slow the effectiveness of the network.

When we see the word *accountability*, we start thinking of micromanagement or overmanagement. This is not the type of accountability that operates in the networked team. The process of accountability for a networked team is centered on the right expectations. Each team member has a particular gift, skill, or talent that they provide to the team. The members are all expected to contribute the maximum effort needed using these gifts, skills, and talents.

Expectations. Accountability is built around expectations, and that, at times, can be dangerous. An adage is that disappointment is in the middle of expectations and reality. When you expect that a teammate will and can perform a specific task or process, a level of trust is built. Of course, there is a level of disappointment when your teammates do not meet their expectations. Discouragement and disappointment can engulf the team unless these three processes are utilized in the networked global teams. They are know, share, and join.

Know. When creating a globally networked team, there is an understanding that each team member knows their strengths and how these strengths fit into the team. The team sees that person as the expert in that area. Networked global teams do not have the time and resources to have team members sitting on the sidelines. They need engaged members exhibiting their strengths in the functions of the team.

Share. The process of being a networked global team is about sharing. As each team member knows their skills, talents, and gifts, they openly share those with the team to grow. There is no withholding these gifts for any reason to promote oneself. Collaboration and service are the cultural norms, not the exception.

Join. The networked global team is an efficient and high-resolution team. The networked global team is centered on everyone joining the process and fully engaging to achieve the objectives. There is no room for teammates to not join in the process and be unengaged. If teammates are not engaged in the process, the network is broken and is no longer the networked global team.

Principles of Global Leadership

The development of global leaders is not an exact science. To start a leadership learning and development process, you first need to describe the core principles for global leaders. They are power (how and when to use it), zeal (dangers of lack of passion), diligence (laissez-faire leadership and inefficiencies), sacrifice (need to self-sacrifice), and compassion (gentle and kind in the development of others). Below are global principles with a brief explanation.

Integrity with power (across cultures). As a global leader expands into an effective leader, the use and sharing of power are critical in measuring effectiveness. The concept of integrity is better identified in a local context. When a person starts leading outside their own culture, it is challenging to identify integrity issues due to language and cultural differences.

Boundaries. One of the most significant challenges global leaders face today is the concept of boundaries. We are experiencing massive refugee challenges stemming from some countries' physical boundaries. From watching the availability of COVID-19 vaccine, we see the challenge of nationalism and the boundaries set up from that concept. We are experiencing trade problems from wanting to keep economic gain inside the boundaries of our countries.

Whether physical, emotional, or cultural boundaries seem to pull us toward our local community, at times, it seems like global leaders are always swimming against the stream. Global leaders have the challenge of influencing people, so they will step out of their natural tendency to the local environment and thrust them into an environment of unknowns, differences, and obstacles. Why would leaders want to treat their followers that way? Why would leaders want to cross boundaries?

The first issue discusses determining the difference between local and global leadership. The debate is over proving the differences between global and domestic leadership. One might ask, why is global leadership an issue? There are three reasons: the need, challenges, and opportunities for global leaders. It is not difficult to understand the need for global leaders who can make the world a better place. The challenge for global leaders is the complexity of leading across cultures. The opportunity is billions of people looking for influential global leaders to serve their villages, communities, countries, and regions.

The global leader is tasked with being able to serve where they are physically while also inspiring and motivating followers in other regions. The global leader sees locally and globally. It is like a person wearing bifocal eyeglasses. The lower part of the glasses allows the global leader to see locally, and the higher side allows a global view.

Example of a Global Leader

The scenario that depicts this description and definition of a global leader is as follows:

Yang grew up in a small village outside Harbin, China, in extreme poverty. Using his determined personality and by achieving high scores on tests, he was chosen to go to a great university in Dalian, China. After graduation, he was introduced to international business and started working for Caterpillar and later AIG. During this process, he learned to speak English, which opened relationships with people outside his culture.

After a few years in business, he decided the needs around Asia were overwhelming and started nonprofit charitable work in 2008 after the Sichuan earthquake. During this time, he built relationships with the US, Europe, the Middle East, SE Asia, and South American leaders. The first step was to create a complex strategy in which he had to identify projects, have a donor network, and build equal relationships across cultures. The outcome of this strategy is sending missionaries to cities around the world.

His implementation was a success, and he became a pastor to thousands worldwide. He utilizes technology like Facebook Live, reaching around 700–1000 people in each event. He also speaks at conferences in multiple countries, which illustrates an equal relationship. All this was achieved by a man who grew up in extreme poverty. It is an example of the foundation and need for global leaders being used for the common good.

Like all electronic mechanisms, the equipment has a power source to work correctly. The networked global team needs a power source to propel the three core areas of shared vision, communication, and accountability. The power source creates the connection that enables each team member to know, share, and join. This can only be done through the principle of integrity.

Part 2

PRINCIPLE 1:
INTEGRITY

When providing examples of integrity, many people focus on ethical or moral decisions in the workplace such as discrimination, physical or verbal abuse, and stealing. These are all great examples, but to me, they do not identify the root cause of the integrity principle. The root cause is centered on the word *power*. Power is part of any discussion on leadership. Although most people see the power in the negative, it is neutral. How the person, leader, or team uses power is how one is graded on integrity.

To live a moral life in any setting needs to start with integrity. There are many definitions for integrity when scanning across cultures, but power is the primary issue we will explore for creating beyond expectations for global teams. The use or abuse of power is the start of the fall of the team and organization. This type of toxicity causes problems that most teams cannot rebound or reorganize around.

The anecdote to this type of toxicity in an organization is humility. For global teams that create a team environment built on empowerment and opportunity, there is humility to guide the principle of integrity. The individual team member understands what makes a person genuinely humble and uses those skills to exhibit leadership. With this process, the individual must learn about boundaries that help the team. This process is generated by humility and is why I call it the power source.

Humility is the power source for the team in how it pushes out toxicity and attracts authenticity and collaboration. From the individual, it leads to the team becoming humble. When the team exhibits humility, the environment becomes conducive to success, especially in a networked or global setting.

As a global consultant, I have seen the good and bad of power in leadership. Those that left a lasting impression on me were the ones that found ways to utilize power to help others. Help could be by providing resources for learning and development, or it could be through encouragement during a specific situation. Often, this happens when people expect a hierarchal or top-down approach but are surprised that the people in power see themselves as servants.

Over the last few years, I have witnessed this in a project for a company that wanted to expand globally. They were very successful in their space for the US market and easily could have copied and pasted their product into other markets worldwide. The copy-and-paste method would be standard for most companies. Why try to fix something that is not broken?

Instead, they created a global team to localize the product. The process was more difficult, but they could do this out of their humility as individuals, teams, and organizations. As I helped build the global teams, the local leader often asked me many questions based on, "Tell me what they want me to do." My reply was, "We are not here to tell you how to build, sell, or market the product to your culture. We are here to serve you as you make these decisions going forward."

This type of humility was always an eye-opening event for the team leader. They now decided on significant issues such as goals and objectives, budget, and staffing needs, and most importantly, they held power in the go-to-market strategy. The client had the power to tell others what to do based on their success in the United States. Still, they saw long-term success built on the fact that they needed to give that power to local leaders while they became servants to achieve the organization's mission.

Chapter 3

HUMILITY: THE POWER SOURCE

A networked global team demonstrates humility. In my experience of observing and leading teams, humility allows a team to grow into a high-performance area. Although humility is often referenced, we must find a way to describe the process of being humble in a networked team.

There is a transparent process to demonstrate humility. The process is the ability to understand each other, be open and authentic to everyone, and follow a greater call beyond their interest.

Ability to Understand Each Other

Teams have become too complex to rely on one hubris leader. For networked teams, leadership will involve a constant shifting of roles as the projects demand agility. To adapt to these changes, a leader understands the team is complex, so they must continue to learn. Part of this learning process is to know what role a humble leader can take in a helping situation. Team members see themselves as a process consultant. In this role, the team members work together to identify and solve problems beyond their expertise. An arrogant leader views success independently from the success of the team whereas a humble leader sees success tied to the team.

The leader learns to ask the right questions to understand each other in the team. By asking for advice, leaders exhibit a form of humility that demonstrates they are open to learning and admit they do not have all the answers. The help is mutual. The leader learns by asking the right questions, and their openness helps the entire team.

Each day, the leader demonstrates humanity, sharing how they face the same triumphs and barriers as everyone. In other words, they refuse the VIP treatment and look to be just one person in the crowd. This openness brings about a connection to each other that strengthens the bond of trust that extends in the network that allows high performance even without being together face-to-face.

Open and Authentic to Everyone

Being open and authentic does not require a person to lose confidence; humble leaders practicing open and authentic traits do not need to prove anything by telling people how good they are. A sense of fairness is formed in the team from being open and authentic, and this trait of humility strengthens the network through the connectivity of trust.

Follows a More Fabulous Call Beyond Their Interest

Humble leaders have to not only understand the complexities of the organization, ask the right questions, connect to others around them, and lead openly and authentically but also focus on something more significant than the self. To develop humble leaders, a person sees organizational transcendence. There is something bigger than one leader or even one group of leaders. Often leaders are described as having their agenda. The plan is not owned by one individual based on their interest but is instead the team's plan and is decided on collectively. The process is team humility. When power and motivation are used with humility, the networked team is so successful.

Chapter 4

TEAM HUMILITY

Why do teams need humility?

The word *toxicity* is used when you listen to any modern business leadership or organizational behavior podcast. The range is from toxic behavior toward other races, genders, or beliefs. The toxicity causes a working environment that is counterproductive to long-term success. High-performing teams need individuals acting with humility to fight off one of the most extensive destructive processes.

Toxic behaviors in a team create an unsafe workplace that is not only about physical safety but also psychological safety. After Google's report was released a few years ago, the word *psychological safety* has grown in popularity. It was one of Google's main focus on what made their team successful. When team members cannot feel emotionally safe, instead of openness and transparency, the team experiences closed and unauthentic or fake behaviors.

For those who serve global organizations in different capacities, toxicity is harder to identify when working across cultures. What is an acceptable norm in one culture might not be the same for another. This complexity causes global teams to suffer when dealing with a safe space to be creative and compelling.

Describe and Identify Toxicity in a Global Team

In research and practice, many names describe a type of leadership that leads to a virus. For example, destructive leadership is a combination of disruptive and toxic leadership. To describe the type of virus that destroys a networked team, "toxic leadership" is the best term. Like a virus, toxic leadership will run through the network and destroy the equipment used to connect the team.

Just as the virus spreads in a network, its ability to break down devices and equipment without notice is alarming to team leaders. Once a toxic leader starts the virus in a networked team, each member is instantly impacted, and most of the time, the members are not even aware the virus infects them. They could become infected and show symptoms instantly, which is the easier identification. Most of the time, the virus is slow to present itself in the network, but the team is compromised and starts to spread the virus in multiple ways. A venomous leader subjects their followers in the organization in the same way.

The virus moves from team member to team member and causes the team process to fail in everyday functions leading to conflict and crisis. When lured by power, control, and financial gain, the problem is that many leaders can go from influential to toxic. For this reason, it is crucial to not only learn about leadership practices but understand the responsibility of being a global leader in identifying the virus even when it comes from those who have been successful in the past.

The Error Code of Toxic Leaders

In my travels worldwide serving organizations, I have been exposed to many toxic leaders. They are constantly looking to subject followers to their toxic virus to control their world, corrupt their surroundings, and construct their own identity. In the process of achieving these goals, they leave followers and fellow leaders discouraged. This discouragement is like an error code destroying the computer's processes until it cannot function. Once they have achieved their goal, the team suffers, and in the long run, the people the team is sent to serve to suffer. Toxic leadership in a team goes way beyond the borders of the team.

Many resources are available to identify the error code produced by toxic leadership. Still, only a few provide a construct on how to identify, Control/Alt/Delete, and reboot after a team experiences a toxic leader. The need for global leaders that can describe, define, and correct the error code is essential to provide research and practical application in dealing with leadership practices that send toxins through the team and organization and disable the vision and mission of the networked team.

An accurate description is needed to understand the benefits of team humility. To this point, the focus has been describing the humility process for the individuals in the team. Team humility is primarily exhibited based on how the team manages power and utilizes motivation to accomplish its goals. A synopsis of what makes a humble team is needed to design a networked global team.

Describing Team Humility

Jim Collins defines the concept of arrogance as "excessive pride that brings down a hero, or outrageous arrogance that inflicts suffering upon the innocent." Arrogance is the opposite of humility, so teams led by arrogant leaders have a higher probability of a toxic atmosphere that makes building a high-performing networked team impossible. There are many examples of how hubris global leaders have destroyed organizations and their teams, but how does humility positively affect organizations? Humility is not a weakness; it is a strength.

There are two primary areas that a networked team must focus on to ensure they have humility in their networked team: power and motivation. I chose these two areas of leadership because most actions come from using power and motivation. Networked global teams that utilize these two practices of humility will have the power to run the team. Still, if the toxic culture of arrogance and pride infiltrates the team, then the team will be running on a low-powered generator at best.

Humility in power

When a networked team needs to demonstrate humility, we start with assessing the use of power. I combine power with an ethos or ethical process in the team that comes from integrity. Why are ethical leadership and integrity complex in global leadership? Because of how the networked team distributes, uses, and demonstrates power during crises and conflicts. Don't assume only destructive consequences in crisis and conflict. We will also explore the constructive consequences while building a foundational knowledge of power and leadership.

One of the primary reasons global leaders are measured by their integrity is because they possess a large amount of power across cultures and countries. Even a small organization in the US that is purchasing and selling its products overseas can influence the community in which they operate. A small business owner in the US can become enamored with power when traveling to a community that treats him like royalty to keep his business. Many theorists believe leadership and power are intertwined and cannot be separated. For this reason, it is vital to understand the good and the bad of power in leadership.

Power needs to be spread around, and control should not be only for a certain few, but the network team needs an even distribution of the share of power to be effective. Like any power grid, the more stations you must share the electricity load, the less probability you will have power outages.

Leadership and power are directly related. Companies face challenges in developing leaders with integrity because authority systems change quickly, and the global economy is moving from a triangle hierarchy to a flat organizational structure. With the increased information provided by technology, having power through the control of knowledge is getting increasingly more complicated.

Humility and motivation

For global teams, there is a constant struggle to create and implement ways to motivate teammates. A hubris global leader usually sides with keeping control while trying to motivate. A humble global leader learns to motivate while giving away control and power. How a person can identify the difference is the intention of the global leader. Are the attempts to motivate coming from an intention to bring praise to themselves, or are the intentions to develop and build up the follower? The most common phrase of this type of action by the global leader is collective.

The global leader in a networked team empowers each other out of shared vision, communication, and accountability. It is not a top-down process of trickle-down ability. Still instead, it is a team holding on to each other, motivating each other to reach new heights, and propelling the organization forward through their leadership. You start with the design to allow maximum power flow through the networked global team.

Part 3

PRINCIPLE 2: PURPOSE

Unfortunately, when people often read the word *purpose,* they think of self-motivation. Motivational speakers often focus on your purpose in life or reason for existing. These are good items but not what helps a team. An individual purpose often harms a team and organization because they do not align and cause operational conflict.

The purpose of a high-performing team is not about the individual benefit. It is about the motivation to lead a group to a higher purpose than the individual. When leading a team, the complexities increase as you build a strategy with purpose across cultures and systems. How do you create a purpose for a diverse team with race, gender, and culture?

The easy answer to this question is to focus on the team and not make it about an individual goal but instead design the team to ensure it keeps a holistic purpose, not an individual one. A design needs to spread power, responsibility, and vision so that each team member feels the purpose is collective and not coming from one or two individuals. A design for teams is tricky and often falls to one or two top performers, and the rest follow with doing the task.

A purpose that leads a team is collective—one that drives every-one to be transformational and go beyond an individual purpose. A collective purpose is powerful and can make changes that impact many people, but a team must be designed to bring out the collective and not the individual.

Chapter 5

THE NETWORK DESIGN

There are a few options when setting up internet and connectivity in your home. The first design option is choosing between land and wireless, which determines the equipment you need. It would be best if you had a hub or router to connect. You can choose the wired option, and you have a wire connected from the hub to your computer, or in some places, the house is wired, and you plug in your ethernet cord to the wall.

A second option is to create a wireless network, so you need a router that takes the internet feed into the house and converts it to a wireless signal. This signal requires devices that can receive the Wi-Fi signal and convert it to operate. The flexibility is incredible, and the devices can roam around, but there are cons. The first is a specific area that binds them. Second, the speed is often slower than the wired network, so communication between devices can cause buffering.

The third option is using what is termed a mesh network. There are many objectives for a mesh network, but for this analogy, we will focus on three. We want the Wi-Fi connection to be as fast or faster than the wired network. We want to be able to expand the network by adding.

We look at a few categories to help global leaders understand which network team is best for their organization. They are speed, agility, efficiency, equipment, and maintenance.

Wired Networked Team (Single Leader Team)

A single team leader model is one that most global leaders still choose—a wired networked team. Many issues lead to this choice, but the primary one is the desire to control the process and keep power. With any decision, the leader has opportunity costs. When you choose a wired team, you gain the most control over any networked team, but you give up speed, agility, and efficiency.

Consequently, the odds that the team will return to being in a working group are very high. Instead of being efficient with a pace to achieve goals that are required of a global team, the team leader will be more focused on keeping costs down due to fewer devices than achieving goals.

So how does this connect to the process of building a Team?

When designing a team, the cost-benefit analysis is a necessary process; all organizations have budgets, and to provide a solution that does not consider cost would be irresponsible of a leader. However, global leaders often choose the wired network because of an issue other than finances: fear.

The fear of the what-if. This fear will prevent a global leader from experiencing the joy of success that only a networked team can provide. If the global leader allows an empowering process to fail, they will look weak or incompetent.

What if we fail?

You can survey 100 leaders, and if they are honest with you, 100 will say they have failed at some point in their leadership. Team leadership is complex; sometimes, we do not do an excellent job with our teams. Failures provide learning moments to build a better team the next time. The disruption to the team from a leader who has a fear of failure is much more damaging.

What if we succeed?

Many leaders fear success more than failure because how do you measure success? What will be required or expected from you in the future if your team is successful? To succeed as a team leader brings attention that causes higher future expectations of the team leader, but through humility, a leader can make sure the team is recognized for success and not themselves. The disruption to the team from a fear of success is sabotage; your decisions and actions aren't providing the positivity needed for the team.

Wireless Network with Single Hub (Networked Team)

Global leaders often want to minimize costs and investment, so they keep the same devices used for the wired network. Once the global leader identifies a need to go wireless, several essential steps exist. The first is you upgrade your system. Not only is this upgrade a financial investment, but it is also a significant time investment.

Also, part of the system upgrade is expanding into a better maintenance program. Once you have invested in the new devices, the wireless program needs regular maintenance. Even in a centrally focused environment, you invest in developing and upgrading your devices that receive the signal.

So how does this connect to the process of building a team?

Purchasing mistakes always stem from knowing what is needed but thinking a cheaper product can be used to accomplish the goal. Global leaders understand they need the speed and agility of a mesh network for the success of their organization, but they are not willing to invest. Again, it is not just about the finances; it is usually more about the time needed to design the mesh network.

Instead, they settle for the off-brand, which looks reasonable—a simple hub that changes from wired to wireless. Their team looks different and, at times, performs at a higher level, but they are not the peak performance. This process could be okay for some organizations, but the leaders who want more settle for the almost great. Again, it is not just cost that keep a global leader from investing in a better team solution, but in the end, it is the need for control. There are two what-ifs from the need to control.

What if they do something wrong?

When expanding cross-culturally, this is a significant issue I repeatedly hear: "Well, my teammates are so many thousands of miles away that I need to keep control, so they do not do something wrong." The disruption to the team with this type of fear brews mistrust and a superiority complex.

What if they are better than me?

The opposite of the fear of something going wrong is what if it goes right. Hubris leader focuses on themselves and wants to make sure they receive the glory for themselves and will keep decisions close so they can own the process. By following this decision-making process, they ensure the team members outside their sphere are not given credit for their work. This type of fear brings the team a sense of disrespect which will quickly end the ability to perform.

Wireless Mesh Network (Networked Global Team)

Once global leaders see the increase in speed, agility, and efficiency from the wireless network, they will start to research how to reach even higher speeds, become more agile, and operate with even greater efficiency. The wireless mesh network provides this option, but the investment needed to convert to a mesh network is usually too high for most leaders.

The leader must add new hubs, and there must be a clear strategy for triangulating the hubs for optimal operations. A single global leader usually can't accomplish this task alone, so it takes help from other resources such as consultants.

So how does this connect to the process of building a team?

When living in Hong Kong, I was always amazed at how many people spent money on sports cars while driving at a maximum of

110km/hr. If I were to spend that much on a car, I would want to ensure I could reach the car's full potential regularly. Similarly, it is the same for the global leader when they choose the power of the networked global team.

The leader has spent the funds. Now, will they utilize the opportunity? The first step is making sure you can invest the proper time. A global leader understands it is a learning process that takes time. The design and setup of a mesh network are not accessible. You test the environment and ensure you have the proper training and development to provide maintenance and care for the product. You have access to reaching high performance. Now can you use your leadership ability to reach the goal?

What if we do not connect?

The entire networked team strategy is based on the ability to stay connected as a team, and if there is no connection, then there is no team. It is, at best, an efficient working group. If a wireless networked team does not connect, then there is no team that is considerable disruption to the organization.

What if we lose connection?

When working using Wi-Fi, we never want to lose the connection because we are disconnected from the world. In the same way, the wireless team makes a connection, and the team is performing at a high level, but then there is a loss of connection. It is not why or how the connection is lost but the fact the communication ends. This is a massive disruption to the team because, like most high-talent people, they move on when disconnected from a project. What do you do next?

Below is a table that provides the three options for global teams.

Table 1.1 explains the difference between single leader working groups and effective teams.

Network Design	Network Global Team with Wired Single Hub	Network Global Team with Single Wireless Hub	Network Global Team with Wireless Mesh Network
Speed (Time frame in which goals are achieved)	Slower process with individual goals that cause projects to slow because each team member has individual agenda.	A faster process because of a shared goal/objectives process but still slows down due to having to constantly return information back to a single hub.	The fastest process of teamwork based on shared goals/ objectives and ability for any hub to transmit information that leads to better and more informed decisions.
Agility (Ability to make changes due to need)	Limited agility due to members working mostly on individual tasks that match their skills. There is a hesitation to reach out for help from others.	Limited agility due to the central focus of the single router/ hub that dispenses major decisions.	Agile team process due to ability to spread out work across routers and with a higher speed bandwidth to make changes.
Efficiency (Ability to complete projects in efficient time and costs)	Less efficient due to work products are mostly assigned to individuals and not as collaborative and chaotic with discussion.	Most efficient because of speed and control of communication from the single wireless hub.	Less efficient because of more parts involved in decisions. This option leads to increased chaos.
Equipment (Talent Acquisition)	Limited need for expensive equipment because the objectives are singular and need for expertise is less which lowers costs.	Limited expenses because most of investment is in the wireless hub that controls decisions and pushes projects.	More expensive because the team needs high-performing hubs, and those devices are costly.

Maintenance (Leader development)	Very little need for maintenance in order to keep operational.	With the requirement of running a wireless network, the team needs maintenance, but it is limited due to most resources are in the wireless hub.	More expensive due to increased amount of equipment that needs serviced.

I use the word *role* when describing the difference between a single leader group and a networked team. In terms of a single leader group, the term role is used like a silo. Often, in these groups, a person will say, "You stay in your lane, and I will stay in mine" type group. "Don't you dare cross over into my expertise." For a networked team, there are still roles, but they are not assigned to one person. They are filled by different people in the network when they are needed, and the teammate could fill the role. The roles are to help the team succeed, not provide tasks to each teammate. Below are some of the essentials.

Energy source. The leadership needed in this role in keeping the team focused on a shared vision. This is more than the person willing to give an inspiring speech; instead, this person can sense when the team is losing focus on the objectives and goals and brings people back to the right point in the process.

Network administrator. Understands what value the team provides to the organization.

Equipment manager. Ability to design and create a structure that provides high-performance, organized process to develop more leaders in the team to achieve higher goals.

How Do Leaders Design Network Teams?

When setting up a home mesh network, the equipment has to be strategically placed to build the most substantial network between the pieces. Global leaders are challenged in many areas when they design a network team. Determining the how, when, and what of the virtual team, which is located across the globe, takes strategic placement.

Below are the options organizations have in building teams.

Option 1. Most employees are local with one central location with individuals remote.

This is a standard option that is not set up for global teams.

Option 2. Most employees are local, with multiple offices in the same country

Again, a prevalent option for local or domestic leaders is to create teams that serve in one country but multiple locations.

Option 3. Most employees are local with multiple global locations.

This option has more complexity because you are dealing in multiple global locations as a team. The excellent point is that the employees are usually from the same cultural background, yet part of the team will live in a different culture. They will experience a different lifestyle that does call challenges for the team.

Option 4. Mostly virtual with employees inside one country.

Over the last two years, with COVID-19, this has become a very prominent design for teams. Companies trying to decide if this is a long-term option for the move to virtual teams have caused much debate on the importance of face-to-face interaction.

Option 5. Mostly virtual with employees working globally.

For the global network team, this is the most commonly used design. The network is virtual, and the people work worldwide to form a diverse, high-performing team.

For the network team, any of these options are open to design, but for the book's focus, we will focus on the virtual and global aspects with option 5. To start designing a virtual team with employees or contractors based in multiple locations, you find the strategic placement of the equipment. The source is nearest to the project. The connectivity needs people on the team that is "central" regarding time zones.

As a scenario, we will use option 5 of a virtual team with members working globally. Below are steps for the design of the network team. (We are jumping to the design part. As explained earlier, the team already has been given the parameters needed to create a team that includes a project with a shared vision.)

Step 1. Decide on the equipment. How many pieces of equipment do you need to create and run the network at a high performance? Working with a mesh network is about placing the equipment in the best location to have the most comprehensive range with the fastest connection. For global teams, that means strategically placing the team in a location that allows for the best productivity for the project. When looking at the project, you decide how many teammates you need to be optimal. How do you decide this number?

To start with, it depends on the size of the project, the agility needed to perform the project, and the speed required to perform the project. Most organizations I've worked with just looked at a cost structure, which is still essential, but the network team focuses on the team's performance, which outweighs the cost. For example, that could mean choosing a highly qualified person out of Singapore instead of hiring three or four people for much less cost out of Indonesia.

Step 2. Decide on the placement of the equipment. There are a few factors that help decide this. The decision on placement begins with understanding the need of the team. Are there specific advantages of being in one area over another? As a leader, you strategically place the team in an area that creates the best opportunity for success. Where and why you place them in that area is essential to communicate. Communication is more than just language. Although the language is essential, it is also about bandwidth for the network. A teammate can slow the performance; again, remember that performance is a crucial indicator for the team, and the teammate can slow performance if they have a slow response and are not placed strategically in the right place to perform the duties and their job.

Step 3. Decide on the type of equipment. In a mesh network, you have the central piece of equipment that creates the network and sends out the signal. Then you have the hubs placed in different rooms. Most networks come with the main piece of equipment and two hubs, but it depends on the size of your house. It is crucial to decide the size of your team because it translates into how many "hubs" you need.

A hub could equal one person, but in global teams, it usually means one or two people per hub. How does a team leader decide how many people per hub? Below is the process for deciding the team investment per hub.

Time. How much time are you providing each team member to complete the process?

Capacity. Each hub requires an understanding of how many units can withstand the network's work. The challenge is how to determine the capacity of each hub.

Once you establish the hub, you need the routers strategically placed around the hub. The challenge is not looking at the routers as just support but seeing them as vital pieces to the team's performance. In the network team, a hub can change to a router. In reverse, a router can move to a hub in a time of need. That means a leader has to be aware of the team's capabilities and place the hub with the right teammate to accomplish high performance during the project. For example, the hub is based in the US. The project requires skill sets that are better served coming out of India. The hub in the US does not try to control or manipulate the situation and still receives the skill sets in India instead of the network team. They passed the baton, you would say, passed the empowerment to the team in India, then became the hub.

This is a critical piece of the network team, and it's so essential for you to see to understand why this book can help you in developing high-performing teams in a networked world. A global networked team is not dependent on one location in one person, but it is networked in a way where you are dependent on each other to strengthen the team.

All these steps described are equally crucial to the global leader in order to create the network. The network allows for the team's design, but now, you are clear on how a networked team operates once it is networked.

Chapter 6

THE NETWORK PROCESS

When we hear the word *team*, most people think of many types of situations, such as sports, work, and church. The problem is that the word *team* is so widely used that it has become a common term to phrase a group of people instead of genuinely describing how a real team operates. Many of us choose a sports team to follow; throughout each season, we see good and bad teams. The team is physically together to meet, practice, play, and perform in each case.

What happens when we no longer have boundaries and use the word *team* in a place where we never physically meet, don't practice together, or build a sense of community from "getting to know" each other? Can we indeed be a team without ever meeting physically? To answer that question, we must look at the dynamics of a team to determine whether we can have effective virtual teams. Can you have virtual teams help us determine how to answer the question? We need to identify the critical dimensions of a team and have a clear understanding of what makes the team effective.

With the world experiencing massive global changes due to pandemics, political unrest, and economic crisis, the ability to define and explain concepts is becoming harder and harder. Most of us will never see the words *social distancing* in the same way after the COVID-19 pandemic.

Outcome

Being a sports team fan would not be fun if we did not keep score to determine who wins. This concept also goes with working in a team. You must be able to keep a score to know if they are performing at their peak. A real team cannot be created and started unless you know when you will be successful. If you are starting a process, there needs to be a clear objective that can be measurable; otherwise, you cannot call that a team. It is just a random group.

The problem is that most leaders need to learn how to keep score of a team's performance. The focus is on individualistic roles and not on the team. There is a place for measuring individuals, but before you start that procedure, you need to have a clear plan to measure the team as a group. There are four steps I recommend to measure the outcome:

1. What is the status of the need? Determine a numerical process to measure where you are currently. Organizations can measure sales for a particular product; others can measure the service in the community. Whatever it is, the leader determines the current situation and why you need a team.

2. Where do you need to go? Teams are critical for the outcome. The leader then sets a goal for the team to achieve. An achievable goal helps propel the organization to a place of success. It isn't easy to achieve success only in working groups.

3. What are the milestones? As you progress, it becomes essential to set milestones to help encourage the team to succeed. When you reach the milestone, celebrate! It is critical for the team. A sports team celebrates after each win. It doesn't mean they are the champions, which are their goal, but each win helps them over toward that outcome. When a leader builds a team focusing on the outcome, it helps set the foundation for success.

4. The next step is understanding that a team only works for a specific period. The leader must determine when the team will begin and when it will finish.

Timing

Teams are not needed regularly. Most of the time, we work in groups that we think are teams because it is an ongoing process that needs a clear goal. To understand high-performing teams, we first explain that a real team has a time limit. It is not perpetual. A team has a specific plan or strategy to accomplish a goal. Once the goal is accomplished, the process returns to a working group until the team creates another plan.

To set up the team for success, the leader determines the team's start. From the process, the team is a better fit for high performance. Three ways can help you determine the start of the team process:

1. *Financial resources.* Before a leader builds a team, they need to assess if the team has the finances needed to succeed. The funds are created for the team to improve the organization so the team convinces top management that it is worth the investment.
2. *Human resources.* The leader determines if the team has the right people to accomplish the outcome. Team leaders connect with other potential teammates across cultures and boundaries, which requires managing the complexities of working across cultures.
3. *Time resources.* Time is a critical piece to team success. The leader properly measures if the team has the time to accomplish the outcome. During the COVID-19 pandemic, we have understood the issue of time resources more than ever. Before the pandemic, we would have our calendars set more than 1 to 2 years in advance. Now, we are lucky to know what we are doing next month. This shorter availability period forces the team to be concise and have a clear vision of goals and outcomes.

People

How does the leader determine the size of the team? The leader determines the team's outcomes and what resources are needed to finish the task. The next step is determining the people on the team. The people on the team process start with determining the correct size. The common mistake is to focus on the roles before determining the size. Instead, the size determines the roles in the team.

A common mistake is to try to have too many people on the team. In sports, you are penalized when you try to add too many people to the match. To play sports more competitively, leagues limit how many people can be on the team. If not, the higher-income teams would dominate all the matches, and the sport would become boring. As a leader, you must think strategically. For this reason, you place the right people with the correct number.

One of the top teams in the world is the Navy SEALs. They choose to work in a team of five to accomplish their mission. You can find many books, movies, or TV series on the SEALs because leaders across all industries can relate to the need to adapt to survive. The SEAL teams believe you have enough roles for the team to adapt, and it is small enough to make fast decisions on the field. If more members were on the team, it would slow down their ability to adapt.

In determining the size of your team, there needs to be an adaptive assessment to help you in the decision. The three essential areas to assess are listed below.

1. *The flexibility needed to accomplish the outcome.* The leader decides if it is a need for the team to adapt quickly to accomplish its goals. If so, the lesser number, the better for adapting. When we dive deeper into the word *flexibility*, we think of the difference between flexible plastic and hard plastic. If you have a hard plastic rod and hit it up against something like a concrete wall, it will break. A flexible plastic, however, when you hit it up against something like a brick wall, will take on that blow when it hits the wall. Similarly, your team needs to be built in a way

that allows the flexible plastic because the team will receive many challenges that will cause them to buckle, but you've got to be flexible to move through those challenges.

2. *The second area needed is determining the roles needed to accomplish the task.* Leaders often only think about the conventional roles of admin finance operations, but these are different from the type of roles I'm referring to. I am referring to the roles needed inside the team and whether the teammates can perform multiple roles simultaneously. Building a team with multiple roles is much more complex, but it gives the team a higher probability of success. Teammates that can perform various roles are critical to the project's success. Leaders often create silos of roles, limiting the amount of teamwork needed for success. Still, in today's world, we no longer can control the processes between finance administration and operations in IT. The environment is all connected, and so we've got to find teams that can function across different roles and different responsibilities to achieve their goals.

3. *The final area to assess the team to determine the size is the environment in which they will work.* Earlier I mentioned the Navy SEALs, who work in a high-intensity environment, so a minor team helps them operate. Still, most of us will never work in that type of environment. Whatever type of environments we work, there is stress, and so we have to look at how stressful it is; if it is a high-stress project, then the more people you have on the team, the more probably you will have people drop out. The type of environment I'm mentioning is one we must choose because of technology.

Once you have a clear outcome/score, a set time to reach your outcome, and the number of people determined, the leader can move to the leadership process. To help describe this process, I will use the term networked team.

To adequately explain a team working in a network, we focus on three critical areas for the networked team. Number 1 is their ability to make effective strategic decisions. Number two is their ability to govern with agility, and number three is the team's ability to develop a future leader.

Strategic Decisions

As we mentioned, the team must focus on outcomes, and part of those outcomes is the ability to expand their ability strategically. In sports, this would be like the underdog winning a championship. The team's function produced the ability to grow, and they expanded their capacity beyond what anyone else could see. This is very important for teams to understand that the goal is not just to be sufficient but to be exemplary.

How can a team grow to exemplary status? The answer is to expand their ability by investing in their capabilities. For a network team, this is going beyond a task. A detriment to most teams is that the day is filled with tasks, and people love to check off tasks from a list without thinking about the implications of what is next for the team. We need more time to think through what is needed to go beyond our expectations as a team. Instead, we stay in mediocrity because that is a safe place for most to be, but for a networked team, you cannot depend on the task because the outcomes require high performance from everyone on the team.

The principle of alignment is critical for determining the strategic decision for teams. What in the world are we doing? As we have established, a team is not set up for ongoing operations but is designed to achieve a specific purpose or goal. For this reason, the global leader determines the strategic direction, such as the team that coordinated landing on the moon.

They had to answer questions like where, how, is it flat, do we have fuel to return? All these are important and how a global team leader views the issues as we advance. Does my strategic decision align with future goals? If so, how does the team's success align with these decisions? The worst strategic decision is not to have alignment with the vision. So all these decision points are critical to the team's success as you go forward.

Team Development

Once this strategic expansion has started, and the team is going or reaching beyond well they ever thought they could do, to further catapult the growth, the networked team must have agile governance. In a working group, the leader creates a hierarchal structure that depends on the top leader to make all decisions. The networked teams can only depend on a simple structure but must be creative and serve in a context that will work in their situation.

Today, everyone talks about the need for agility, and indeed, COVID-19 has taught us that need, but in a sense, it also becomes a buzzword or fad. There are key points to being agile, and it's not solely about making decisions. It is who's making the decisions and who has control. There is always a need for a captain on the team—one that would inspire, provide security, and create systems and processes that allow the team to grow. Still, in a networked team, that person does not necessarily hold all the power and decision-making, ultimately leading to control.

For a networked team to become high-performing, the agility of the governance is one where everyone freely and securely can provide input into decisions in control. The problem is that most traditional leaders do not want to give up decision-making and control. They have the headquarters structure and governance where everything looks back to a centralized point. They are people sitting in the exact location and making the primary decisions. The networked team cannot operate under this type of governance.

Nothing allows for greater agility than a global team appropriately designed to meet the project's goals and adapt to changes in current environmental requirements. During the COVID-19 pandemic, I led teams worldwide with our operational headquarters in Singapore, but Singapore's strict lockdown laws led the team to decide there had to be flexibility in location in order not to stop operations. The best option was to start another organization in UAE, which was friendlier to businesses remaining open, and share responsibility with the Singapore office.

Leadership Development

A team needs a seasoned global leader to operate in this type of process where you perform strategic expansion and agile governance. We know from research that seasoned global leaders are few and far between. For this reason, the network team has always been focused on leadership development.

Networks can only have a long-term impact if they develop leaders. Up to 80 percent of leadership development is based on experience. The need for leadership experience is especially true for adults, who usually lead teams and organizations, so it is easy to say that you give people the leadership experience to develop. This one of the agile governances is so important because it places everyone in the team in situations where they will be leaders so they can gain leadership experience.

Recently Tom Peters tweeted out that 70–85 percent of the workforce needs to be more engaged. He then asked what leaders are going to do about this problem. For global leaders, the problem is identifying if they are engaged and trying to find ways to measure engagement while not seeing the team regularly. To accomplish this goal, it takes the Nextgen Global Leader.

The Nextgen Global Leader doesn't mean you need to hire younger people or people with a better knowledge of current technology. Instead, it is about a process that uses systems and processes across cultures and boundaries to create high-performing teams. For the networked team, it is about creating antivirus software to keep the virus from penetrating and destroying the team's function.

Strategic direction, team, and leader development are critical components of the team's function. To understand how to make these parts of the teams exemplary, we must first look at the viruses that can stop the networked team from learning how to create antivirus software to identify and root out the virus.

Part 4

PRINCIPLE 3: SACRIFICE

What comes to mind when you think about your greatest fear? For me, it is landing in a pond of crocodiles or being closed in with snakes or spiders. When discussing fears with leaders, the most common fear is failure. Therefore, leaders turn to management to try to limit the possibility of failure, which unintentionally causes chaos in the team as management skills cannot replace leadership.

The leader or leaders in the team must understand the principle of sacrifice to lead in a way to help the team become high-performing. The principle of sacrifice starts with the willingness of the leader to see past their fears to face the challenges for the team. When they are choosing to manage during challenging times instead of leading causes a peace disturbance to the team.

When a leader acts and sacrifices beyond their fears, this does leave them in a vulnerable place. The result of this action is what the team needs. You see more engagement and motivation from the team due to the sacrifice made by the leader. When the team is more engaged and motivated, it allows them to be high-performing instead of in conflict and lack of peace, and in today's world, that quickly leads to quiet quitting.

In sports, we see this often for championship teams. Leaders sacrifice for the team's good instead of being concerned about failures. A great example that comes to mind is the sacrifice Hinds Ward made for the Steelers to move to a new position, and he became a leader on the team that went to the Super Bowl multiple times.

The principle of sacrifice is easy to identify. The issue is the action. Will the leader be courageous enough to think beyond their fears for the team to be successful? The best way to describe this process is to show that the greatest fear for the network is a virus. How do leaders stop a virus from damaging the entire system?

Chapter 7

THE NETWORK FUNCTION

Over the past few years, we have witnessed this fear (virus) used for military bases, oil pipelines, and more. Fear is created with scenarios such as a virus infecting an airplane or car network. There should be similar fear of a virus when working as a networked global team. You have the usual viruses for a traditional team, but there are unique ones for the networked global team that can disturb, slow, and eventually destroys the team's performance. I term this virus as destructive leadership. Many people see the words *destructive leadership* and think only about one person with a title, but within the networked global team, destructive leadership can come from any team member.

The type of virus that disturbs, slows, and destroys a globally networked team is toxic leadership. For a networked team, a virus is toxic, and the toxicity is devastating to the network for many reasons. The primary reason is connectivity. In a network, a virus can spread quickly because of the need to stay connected to everyone on the team. A virus can be stopped in a traditional office setting because of daily personal interaction with each team member. Still, for a networked team, the virus can stay hidden for a particular time. The first sign of a possible virus is a disturbance of the peace.

Disturbance of Peace

As a hacker would secretly try to inject a virus into a computer network, toxic leaders use a similar type of stealth method. Often, a disturbance of peace is not a full-blown conflict in that people identify the virus at the beginning, but the disturbance happens slowly. It is like a computer starting to shut down or lock up without reason. For a networked team, when becoming infected with a virus, they experience lower productivity, minor conflicts, and a lack of motivation. The networked team needs leaders that can identify these issues and start to correct them with antivirus software. To help teams with the antivirus, we must first learn what a potential virus looks like by being able to describe it adequately.

Describing a Potential Virus

When one thinks of destructive leaders, we often think of dictators that brought about large genocides. These leaders used tyrannical power to influence followers and were relentless when someone opposed their views. These highly destructive behaviors exist in governments, companies, and teams, but they are not the type we usually see in networked teams. The more prevalent virus is a passive behavior that damages more teams than you can imagine. The term *destructive leader* is still new in empirical research as most leadership is described in constructive behaviors. Still, more research has described destructive behaviors over the last ten years.

Some of the most influential research into destructive behavior is produced by Einarsen—the destructive behavior grids. In the grid, there are four behaviors. Two are passive, and one is aggressive. Passive behaviors disrupt and destroy organizations and teams more than blatant aggressive behaviors.

To destroy the unity of the team is tyranny in destructive leadership. In these passive behaviors, there are the passive-aggressive who have a plan. They use passive communication to manipulate the team into their beliefs instead of using their leadership to unite them.

This behavior is identified and dealt with immediately, or if the virus of tyranny can spread, it could be the team's end.

Tyrannical Destruction of the Networked Team

Tyrannical leadership practices in a team undermine the goals and objectives. When a team member can disrupt the vision of the outcome, the network is slowed and useless to the organization. Einarsen writes,

> The motivation, well-being, and job satisfaction of subordinates without necessarily being destructive regarding the organization's goals. Tyrannical leaders may achieve goals, tasks, missions, and strategies of the organizations, but they typically obtain results not through but at the cost of subordinates.

A challenge to network teams is identifying passive destructive behaviors. Passive toxic behaviors show consideration for the team's goals. This is what makes the virus so dangerous because these behaviors are not aggressive bullying or terrorizing behavior, but they still undermine the goals and objectives of the team. Most networked teams do not have apathetic/laissez-faire type of leaders. Instead, the practices of toxic leadership look like they are great team members, but the virus they are infiltrating into the network is highly destructive. How then do you see the error codes in the network?

Chapter 8

IDENTIFY THE VIRUS

In the current global environment, there are many conversations around the abuse of power, thievery, and discrimination. These are, of course, very toxic behaviors in any team. Still, from my research and practical experience, viruses are often not injected into a team by just the prominent destructive practices described in mainline news reports. Those are usually the extremes. An underlying practice causes the most significant problems and can come from the unluckiest resources. For this reason, the first step in the process is proper identification. The identification process comes with the description and definition of toxic leadership that we have provided.

The identification process is tricky. All teams go through challenges, and leaders cannot constantly think that there is a virus when anything negative happens. For this reason, a global leader uses contextual intelligence to make sense of the situation to identify if there is a virus. Sweet and Beck define contextual intelligence as "the ability to accurately diagnose a context and make the correct decisions regarding what to do." A more straightforward definition is the ability to "read the signs and know what to do."

A word like *contextual intelligence* sounds complicated. There is a reason for that when determining causes and problems across a network that expands multiple countries. The challenge is highly complex. To identify the virus in the network, there are a few steps to help remove some of the complexity. The global leader shows contextual intelligence by first reading the signs. In this case, the team leaders identified that there was a virus. Below is a list of a few signs that a virus has infiltrated the network.

Not Caring for Team Goals/Outcomes

Apathy is a sign and most critical of viruses that a leader needs to be able to identify. If a network is infected with a virus that causes the team members to stop caring about reaching goals and achieving the outcomes, the team has to quickly remove the virus.

A team that has built trust and a strong bond finds identifying this sign of a virus challenging. The default process is to trust the team's process to endure the challenges. For this reason, the team needs to understand the difference between a team and a working group. A team has a specific purpose for a particular time, and that purpose cannot be clouded by apathy.

Losing Direction

A virus that causes almost as much destruction as apathy is losing direction. Even an efficient team and one with unity and cohesiveness are lost if going in the wrong direction. The team keeps track of progress to identify the sign of losing direction.

The virus of losing direction happens when a team stays emotionally connected but stops measuring results. The team "feels" like it is doing great, but it could be losing the direction sending them to reach its purpose. A viruslike losing direction is a gradual infection after a team has bonded.

Wrong People on the Team

A team can have a clear direction and a solid strategy to achieve goals, but if the wrong people are on the team, the virus will slow down and even destroy momentum. Identifying this virus is difficult when the team depends on one person to make the hiring decisions. The other team members start to allow one person to form the team around people like the one leader and not the diversity that the team needs.

This virus is easier to identify but difficult to change. Removing a team member is always tricky but adding that at least one member on the team does not see the person as the wrong one creates more challenges. Because of this dynamic, the virus can grow and infest the team in damaging steps.

Control/Alt/Delete

After proper identification, a leader or follower or both must respond appropriately to the virus. Even though I've been using an Apple product for 15 years, I still remember how to Control/Alt/Delete a PC. It is like when we restart a mac. When using Control/Alt/Delete, you are attempting to erase the flawed processes on the PC to make it run more effectively.

When a virus is identified, the team quickly reacts to keep the performance at a high rate. The worst thing to do is to identify the virus and not try to restart the team. The team must respond to the virus and cannot overlook the virus and allow the virus to stay. With a thinking process, the virus will eventually get better on its own. A network doesn't ever work to the best performance with a virus.

Unfortunately, most teams in an organization have identified the virus being injected into the network but look the other way. The destructive path left by the virus causes teams to become dysfunctional, and rarely do they meet their goals. They start moving from being a team to just being a group. These groups can function many times, but they never reach the goals and objectives of a high-performing team. So how does a team reset when they identify a virus?

Below is the list I used to explain the types of viruses in a networked team. I will use each to give examples of how you reset the team when this virus is identified. The primary question for hitting Control/Alt/Delete is when and how I reset the team. Watching sports over the years has helped me see this happen. Great coaches have a way of "waking up" their players. This process is a reset. Sometimes, they use a player-only meeting, or other times, it is doing nothing when the team expects a punishment. Either way, contextual intelligence is needed to make that decision in a networked team.

Of course, there are many more ways to reset. My goal in this exercise is to provide ideas to help you going forward.

Ways to Reset the Team

Not caring for team goals/outcomes

Explanation. Apathy is the first and most critical of viruses that a leader needs to be able to identify. If a network is infected with a virus that causes the team members to stop caring about reaching goals and achieving the outcomes, the team quickly removes the virus.

When to reset. A team misses its mark many times. For most teams, we sometimes set the goals too high, or unforeseen circumstances stop us from reaching our goals. But when the team is not reaching goals under normal operational circumstances, and there are repeated excuses for not reaching their goals, you think there is a virus, and there needs to be a rest.

How to reset. This option is a tricky one. Apathy almost calls for the immediate removal of the entire team, but a team can reset before one tries the nuclear option. There are many options for a team-building exercise to determine why apathy has crept into the team, but whatever is used, the team is seeking renewal. A renewal that refocuses the goals and outcomes identifies the apathy virus and removes it.

Losing Direction

Explanation. A virus that causes almost as much destruction as apathy is losing direction. Even an efficient team and one with unity and cohesiveness are lost if going in the wrong direction. To identify the sign of losing direction, the team has to keep track of progress.

When to reset. Teams don't have to create mission statements and repeat them daily. It is mundane and boring. There must be a way to measure if the team understands the mission to determine their ability to know if the team is heading in the right direction. If teams are unaware of the mission and cannot identify their direction, it is time for a reset.

How to reset. One of the best ways to reset is to refocus. Some teams like to retreat or take a day away from the office. Whatever the process, the outcome of the exercise should be the same. It is time to refocus the team to ensure everyone understands the direction they are going to reach their mission/vision.

Wrong people on the team

Explanation. A team can have a clear direction and a solid strategy to achieve goals, but if the wrong people are on the team, the virus will slow down and even destroy momentum. Identifying this virus is difficult when the team depends on one person to make the decisions. The other team members start to allow one person to form the team around people like the one leader and not the diversity that the team needs.

When to reset. A high-performing team utilizes the expertise of everyone on the team, but even the best of teams has onlookers at times. When the virus of the wrong people sets in the team, the number of onlookers increases, and ultimately, everyone is usually just watching and waiting on one person. This means it is time for a reset.

How to reset. The first step is returning the work to the team. The person everyone has been watching stops doing the work and controlling the processes and instead gives the work back to the team. At that point, if there are still onlookers, those would need to be removed one by one with a clear explanation to the team. The removal is not the reset. The reset comes when you bring on new team members that are experts in the area of need.

Judgment instead of grace

Explanation. In a networked environment, there is an easy opportunity to judge the actions of your teammates. The judgment comes in passive behaviors that cause trust issues and disunity. This virus is not as toxic but spreads much faster and infiltrates the team in a way that causes relational problems. These relational problems across the network are not seen clearly because it is a network and not in person.

When to reset. Critiques are part of any team process. We need feedback and constructive criticism. The focus is on the word constructive. Criticism always needs to be in a way that builds people up. When criticism in the team becomes destructive and tries to belittle teammates, it is time for a reset.

How to reset. An American terminology used in many organizations is a "come to Jesus" meeting. The meeting is when the grievances are aired, and a correction is made. The team comes together, forgiving each other, and criticism starts moving from destructive to constructive. This happens when people are fed up with the judgments and need grace.

Part 5

PRINCIPLE 4:
DISCIPLINE

When sitting around the dinner table, there are plenty of opinions on what needs to change in the family, community, nation, and world. Everyone has thought about what needs to change, but very few people can make change a reality in the way that a leader in a global team can. Because of the complexities and challenges of leading a high-performing global team, there will always be ideas of what needs to change, but very few can come up with the idea, plan, and implement the change to see it as a success.

The process of creativity, planning, and implementation are all factors that require discipline, which is our principle for global leaders. Discipline is an aspect of self-control. Being able to structure priorities for different teams around the world to know when and how to lead change takes a unique global mindset. A global leader takes time to make sense of the world. There is a challenge for the global leader to stay disciplined while adapting to the fast-paced global environment. The ability to lead change is unique. The ultimate test of discipline is the self-control to manage pain and remedies to make change successful.

The key concept for leading a global team with discipline is the ability to properly diagnose when change is needed and then prescribe the solutions accurately. I label this process for a networked team as being able to do a Control/Alt/Delete to the system. This is not a micro change for the team; macro challenges exist. The action could cause some to leave, be asked to leave the team, or purchase new equipment for the system.

Identification and scanning for a virus are how we term the process of diagnosis and prescribing. Researchers such as Ronald Heifetz believe this is the only role for leaders during a crisis, and everything else is management. If so, the principle of discipline only takes on more of a critical process for global teams.

Chapter 9

THE INFECTION

The team has identified the virus and decided to reset with a Control/ Alt/Delete, and now what. To give you the best explanation, I will use a situation to provide an example. The situation is based on how crises can speed up the spread of the virus. A virus needs a catalyst. Simply, it needs someone to click the link to infiltrate the network. A crisis is an email, and the team clicks the link during the crisis. This speeds up the virus entering the network.

For almost two years, we have been experiencing a global crisis with a pandemic and global economic challenge. All these situations have been taxing to globally networked teams. With this current crisis, global leaders cannot afford to have ineffective or inefficient organizations. The problem is that most organizations are stuck in survival mode during crises such as COVID-19 and have no plans or strategy for moving beyond. This approach is like playing with fire, in which most organizations are burned. The challenge for net-worked teams is to reflect and learn how to create an environment that thrives in crisis and does not allow a virus to spread.

A crisis that we have experienced brings about many viruses. People are stressed, depressed, fatigued, and angry at the circum-stances. For these reasons, it would be silly to think organizations and teams will not have one or two viruses in the network. For cri-sis, the question is not if but when the virus will enter the network. When the virus is sent into the network, there are challenges for the team. The challenges lead to a slowdown in team performance impacting the organization, shareholders, stakeholders, and anyone associated with the product.

The global pandemic crisis has increased the need for global leaders to create networked teams that are high-performing. At a time, when the world is seeing natural disasters, poverty, human trafficking, and many other social challenges, the pressure on social change for global leaders to perform at a high level is coming from donors, boards, partners, and, most of all, the needy in the communities. A compassionate leader will see these needs and understand to help people. It would help if you built a culture in an organization that is effective, efficient, and exceeds what is thought possible. The need for motivation across generations starts with creating an organizational culture that reaches everyone.

As organizations face the crisis with so many unknowns, how do teams operate across regions, cultures, and companies while trying to keep authority and control of systems and processes while allowing for the flexibility required to react to constant changes in their communities, countries, and global markets? How do global leaders create teams with a culture that decreases the possibility of virus infection during crisis events?

The weakness of the hierarchical structure places pressure and stress on one or two leaders. It creates an environment of narcissism which leads the top management teams to make decisions that provide individual benefits and not what is best for the group. A PricewaterhouseCoopers study of the millennial generation in the workplace shows that 85 percent desire development over anything else when starting a new job. Dissemination of knowledge throughout the organization is seen as a strength. The spread of knowledge means organizations release specific power and authority to a younger workforce which causes a dilemma in organizations as they rethink their authority structure. Do organizations open the opportunity to create teams for leadership for all? Or do they limit the number of people who know to keep control? Attempting to control knowledge and authority is a pressing issue on the modern period's traditional, hierarchal organizational chart.

Leaders in organizations are meeting multiple challenges with the complexity of global demands and multigenerational and cross-cultural leadership. The opportunity for a leader to exhibit destructive behavior increases as the temptation to abuse power through wrongful or toxic behavior increases. The destructive behavior comes from abuse of power, bad ethical decisions, and cognitive inability. The toxic behavior is more pronounced during a crisis. To show the impact of a virus during a crisis, we must first explain what an organizational crisis is and how to identify the problems and opportunities for solutions.

Organizational Crisis

An organizational crisis is when organizations need to speed up decisions that do not have the time and other resources available during normal operations. Crisis events are low probability, low frequency events threatening the organization's survival and the goal of achieving the vision. By not achieving the organization's goals, a crisis event is a disruptive event that challenges the organization's endurance to exist and continue toward the organizational vision.

Many events bring conflict to organizations regularly. Regardless of whether the crisis event is caused by humans or nature, it can cause devastating consequences to the vision and mission of the organization. For this reason, it is surprising that more research is not focused on the type of leadership needed to lead an organization through conflict and crisis.

Crisis management causes many problems inside the organization. The difference in exigencies between leaders and managers is seen when groups face crises. A crisis is the turning point for the group. In this turning point, the leader is responsible for either absolving the group or transforming it through the crisis. Even though management is needed, the leader's communication is the most vital part of steering the group in the right direction.

The actions of leaders are where many research hours were invested. Over the years, many leadership theories have been presented as the best type or style of leadership. Out of all these theories, one item has remained the same: the aspect of power has something to play in leaders' actions. Power is an essential piece in determining how leaders act during a crisis.

One of the critical philosophical discussions in leadership continues to be in knowledge and power. With knowledge comes power; therefore, as leaders hold power, what knowledge should they give and withhold from their followers? Recent business failures have shown how large corporations failed because of a small group of rogue employees who withheld knowledge to gain power and authority, and they ultimately caused the demise of the organization. By examining the interaction among knowledge, power, and authority in organizations, the question is not if power is part of leadership but how a person receives power, and how does the leader utilize this power?

When a leader obtains power, there is a change in the leader's life, and power can become a type of addiction leading to an effort of some leaders to hold onto power. The fear of loneliness and depression magnifies the actions of leaders if power is lost. The use of power is prevalent when organizations experience a crisis. During events that lead to crisis, organizations are faced with leaders' behaviors that either cause destruction or can turn the crisis into an opportunity. Heifetz exerts that leadership is most effective in a crisis. Greenleaf distinguishes power for servant leaders as legitimate power that is asserted through persuasion, not coercion.

As society and businesses grapple with the change from a modern to a postmodern society, the issue of the distribution of power continues to be debated, especially with the tendency to control power during a crisis. The question about a leader having power has been answered affirmatively. The main question now is how the leader distributes the power.

Crises are all too much every day due to the complexities facing organizations. The problem is, what type of leadership is needed for organizations to navigate through the crisis? Research shows that organizations tend to withdraw knowledge and power from confident few leaders during a crisis, which can lead to organizational vulnerability.

What Causes Crisis?

The first time anyone visits Phnom Penh, Cambodia, they usually tour a museum that recognizes the horrors of the genocide of the Khmer Rouge. The first time I visited was horrible, but the challenge was the last time I had my thirteen-year-old daughter with me. Try explaining why someone would kill 2–3 million people. The problem is that some museums or places commemorate horrendous acts of violence and death anywhere you go worldwide.

When I walked the grounds of Auschwitz in Poland, there was an overwhelming feeling of knowing the horrors of death, pain, and destruction, of course, or extreme examples. Still, we can think of situations where we experienced hurt in our work or personal life in which a person we trusted caused us to hurt. These leaders chose to focus on themselves and not on the good of others. They are destructive to their organizations, communities, and families. I like to describe them as venomous leaders.

For organizations, the COVID-19 pandemic has caused a crisis which is an understatement in many ways. The COVID-19 pandemic caused an economic crisis which has led to social unrest. All these instances by themselves cause low probability and low-frequency events. When you add all the situations created by COVID-19, it becomes a once-in-a-generation crisis, which we hope we do not see again in our generations.

To provide content to a situation created during the crisis, we can give a formal definition, and from that definition, we can synthesize the organizational crisis with the issues of a networked team.

A more detailed definition of organizational crisis is when organizations encounter a unique, threatening, and stress-inducing decision-making environment that requires consistent attention promptly.

Unique, threatening, and stress-inducing environments

Organization. Like any organism, a group cannot always stay under high stress. Humans are given adrenaline to help us in high-stress events. Adrenaline is a temporary hormone; if prolonged, it could hurt the body instead of help. It is the same for organizations. Employees eventually suffer under pressure if we stay on high urgency during a crisis. We see this now after a year and a half of uncertainty with COVID-19. Organizations have caused many problems by keeping a high threat level.

Networked team. Much like the organization, the networked team cannot survive long-term in a highly urgent environment without constantly keeping high alert. Unlike organizations, teams can survive better in this environment because teams and their goals are short-term. If a team had been created for a one-year project, they would have worked in a crisis environment for the entire project. Like the military, you periodically remove the team members from assignments to reenergize for the next project.

Decisions that require constant attention

Organization. Even a small organization makes many decisions a day. These decisions are monitored during a crisis, but as the organization grows, it becomes harder and harder to provide constant attention. At times, the critical decisions in a crisis will be wrong. How does the organization handle wrong decisions? Many of the mistakes are that the organization doesn't have organizational leadership who can network to solve the problems.

Networked team. Effective networked teams benefit the organization greatly in this way. A networked team will be more efficient in monitoring decisions and correcting them. Their ability to be agile and make corrections to the decision is an advantage. They also have more knowledge because they are "on the ground." Organizational decision-making during a crisis is too slow and has limited knowledge. The organization needs networked teams to have the ability to help with critical decisions. The crucial part for organizational leaders is to decide what critical decisions to assign to the networked teams.

Decisions that are made on time

Organization. Organizations are never timely. Even the most agile organizations are slowed as they grow, so there is always a challenge of making decisions promptly. The COVID-19 crisis has shown this challenge as larger organizations cannot decide how and when to return to an office. When making decisions within a time-frame, organizations need help, and that is where networked teams provide support.

Networked team. Making well-informed decisions promptly is the advantage for the networked team. The team is structured in a way to make effective, timely decisions. When you add the diversity of the team, a team-based approach to decisions, and the fact that all are decision-makers, it adds up to a great advantage for the organization. The critical part is that it allows the networked team to make timely decisions. Organizations cannot force the teams to operate under the same system that keeps their decision-making slow, especially during a crisis.

Drilling down to a more specific situation within the crisis helps provide a situation for you to compare to your crisis management. Notice how the crisis of the organization causes issues for the networked team, but the global leader uses different processes to help the team stay focused during the crisis.

The Situation: A Multigenerational Workforce During a Global Pandemic

An individual or team cannot constantly work in a crisis. Many have used the four tables to describe a process, and many have used the words like *a sense of urgency*. Individuals and teams can only stay in urgency mode for a long while before they cannot function. Look at nurses in hospitals; they are constantly in crisis mode, but urgency only happens in special moments. The important aspect of organizational leadership is understanding how long the individuals and teams can be in urgency mode.

An example of the type of crisis many organizations and teams are facing is the COVID-19 global crisis. With the need to expand to virtual-only meetings and processes, the crisis left many in the team without proper development. We were already experiencing some workforce issues before the COVID-19 crisis, but it has been exponentially worse with a multigenerational workforce. As we look at the crisis and specific situations, it is essential to see how networked teams help organizations in crisis.

Unique, threatening, and stress-inducing environment

Organization. A threatening and stress-inducing environment is complex in a multigenerational workplace. When a crisis like COVID changes how we work and live, it causes many problems for organizations. Although there are up to five generations in some organizations, we will look at the three largest below.

Baby Boomers (born between 1946–1964)

This generation felt left out during the crisis. They had to learn how to Zoom or utilize Microsoft Teams. They are close to retirement, but COVID delayed many, so their plans have significant stress. They have a threat to their day-to-day working conditions and stress related to learning new ways of communicating and maybe losing their retirement plans. The stress of change during the pandemic has left them discouraged and distant.

Generation X (born between 1965–1980)

This generation waited years for the Baby Boomers to retire so they can finally move up the career ladder. With the changes during the crisis, they have felt threats to their plans not only from the potential delay in baby boomers' retirement but the fact that the younger generation can excel in the new environment better than they do. The stress of change and the pandemic has left them uninspired and unengaged.

Generation Y/ Millennials (born between 1981–2000)

This generation is excited about the changes, and they enjoyed working from home. They are accustomed to being connected to a device 24-7. They can play more in nature, or some have decided to move away to the rural areas to enjoy life. As organizations look past COVID, they are rethinking the "virtual" model and requiring some to return to the office. This generation is stressed by the threat to their new freedom and is not in a hurry to return to their old cubicle.

Networked team. The chaos in a crisis of a threatening and stressful work environment is a problem for most, if not all, organizations. How do they approach the issues explained above? There are a few areas that networked teams help with the area of threats and stress in the work environment. They are retention and planning for the future.

Retaining top talent during the crisis has been an issue for many organizations. With more people in "free agent" mode, employees have been jumping around companies looking for the best arrangement. The old career path of working 15–20 years at a company is not an option for Gen X. So what kind of work environment and practices do we have to drive retention for each generation?

Communication. People who work across cultures are more diverse and feel more at ease communicating in a different context. The key to the skill is understanding what type of communication is needed. This skill is in great demand when working across generations during a crisis.

A high-performing networked team is built to plan, focusing on goals and high performance. They find it easier to acquire top talent with a low retention rate because of a desire for engagement. Tom Peters tweeted that a year and a half into COVID, global organizations only have about 30 percent engagement from their employees. The unengaged leave without notices and perform at low levels. Because of the nature of networked teams, everyone is engaged, driving higher-retention during crisis events.

Decisions that require constant attention

The next part of a crisis is the constant attention needed on decisions. When leaders express decision fatigue, there are more issues across generations. Below are a few examples.

How are decisions made?

Baby Boomers. They have seen the introduction of computers to the workplace. They had to learn how to send an email and what it meant to stay connected. The world continues to change, and there is more demand to make decisions with constant attention in the current crisis. Baby Boomers are comfortable with individual decisions, but with the virtual team progression, they are now forced to collaborate.

Generation X. Most of the generation has only known a workplace with a computer that allows email connectivity. Even with this knowledge, they used to have hours, if not days, to respond to decisions with email. Over the last few years, communication has shifted away from email and more to a quick burst of information with limited context. Making decisions with constant attention is difficult for Gen X because some decisions do not allow for a delay in an email response.

Generation Y/ Millennials. This is another example of how this generation is more skilled to flourish in this crisis environment. Their biggest challenge is how to communicate with the other generations in a way that will help keep a constant attention to decisions. The other generations will feel behind and discouraged if they push too hard with limited information.

Networked team. Crisis events in an organization increase stress in many ways. The local situation dictated if the organization was in crisis in the headquartered work environment. For a networked team, members can be in crisis for different times and reasons. They are accustomed to making decisions that require consistent decisions.

How do networked teams reduce the urgency in constant attention to decisions during a crisis? Cultural change.

During crises, the high-stress environment causes conflicts and disputes when the old system is not changed. Times like COVID-19 have made organizations make a culture change to their work process and how they make decisions. These cultural changes are complex, but the networked team helps navigate the challenges by the following:

- *Adaptability.* A networked team has been high performing across generations before COVID. They will surely flourish because they are accustomed to adapting to the changing global environment.
- *Focused attention.* A networked team is high performing because they keep constant, focused attention on decisions. It is in their nature to have multiple people collaborating to make important decisions. During the crisis, the networked teams naturally model the process of this type of decision-making process.

Decisions that must be made in a timely manner

Along with the fatigue of constant attention to decisions, the added stress of decisions being made on a clock is difficult. Even a seasoned NFL quarterback forgets about the clock when making pre-snap decisions, or the best NBA shooters look foolish trying to shoot as the shot clock is expiring. Time-based decisions can make us all look like amateurs, and when you add making time-based decisions across generations, it is comical as a spectator but horrendous when in the middle of it. Below are a few examples:

Balance and workload

Baby Boomers. This generation does not understand the need to balance life. They will keep grinding at work and pushing decisions that can be positive and negative. The positive is that they will push decisions. The negative is that they will push beyond limits and cause discouragement.

Generation X. In many cases, they are the hybrid generation that can connect to baby boomers and Gen Y. They see the benefits of working as a peacemaker in the organization, but this also can cause this generation to become laissez-faire.

Generation Y/Millennials. In many ways, this generation has benefited from changes due to COVID restrictions. A more balanced work-life allows for freedom. This has led many to say the work week should be only four days. Also, this generation is pushing for more control when they are on the job.

Networked Team. Balance and workload cause issues within the same generation and cultures. When working through a network and virtually, most people do not have the standard 8:00 a.m. to 5:00 p.m. workweek. Some cultures cut the workweek to 4 days while others still work 6 to 7 days a week. The challenge for a networked team is to find balance within the team that is a mixture of generations and cultures. When you add the pressures of multiple generations and cultures, the challenge almost seems insurmountable for leaders of teams.

How do networked teams reduce the stress of balance and workload?

Respect local cultures. Nothing shows hegemony more than when one culture says their holidays are essential and others are not. I have heard many explanations ranging from the standard holiday to the region taking too many holidays. Or, on the other end, these guys work all the time, and they are never off. It isn't easy to match their production. The solution for the networked team is to learn to balance out the workload for each team member to stay engaged. This type of balance starts with a leader being culturally aware of how each team member approaches a workload balance.

Learn to say no. Respecting cultures does not mean you say yes to every request. At times, cultures constantly ask you to do work even on weekends and holidays. It is usual for them to ask; they are not trying to disrespect you, but in the end, you must be comfortable with the team to say no.

Work smart. In the end, it is about performance, and the networked team focuses on working wise and can learn to be flexible to adapt to the workload balance of each team member.

Leadership development

Any organizations desire for their employees to develop. The development process should lead them to become leaders in the organization and team. It is from this pool of leaders that networked teams are created. The challenge is that leadership development is viewed differently between generations, and the perception is essential to the program's ultimate success.

Baby Boomers. They see leadership development as an honor of selection, reserved only for a certain number of people; if selected, one should be recognized and even receive their picture on the wall. The expectation and perception are that the leadership development program is formal and detailed with professional teachers. The process is long and almost equivalent to receiving a master's degree.

Generation X. Again, this generation is the in-between generation. They still want a formal learning and development process, but they have also been introduced to experiential learning. They want a process in which they receive the honor, like the baby boomers, but they also want direct experience with the learning process. They used words like management trainee program or interim director during their learning process. They sat through formal learning classes while also being sent worldwide to experience leadership in other cultures. Through all this, they learn to be the person between generations.

Generation Y/Millennials. Recently, there was a significant investment in a new learning app for organizations. The app is receiving a large amount of attention. It is used for multiple ways of learning, but leadership development is one of the processes. The significant aspect is the learning is peer-to-peer. You can share a lesson with someone above, below, or equal to you in the organization. The objective is that the app will build a learning community. I am not here to determine if this is the correct way of developing leaders, but it does shine an ample light on generational differences in the workplace regarding learning and development.

Networked Teams. For networked teams, there is the challenge of how you mix the learning and development programs to serve the team members. If you make it formal, then you will lose the younger generations. Suppose you choose learning and development solutions in which millennials expect skill development in return for delivering high-quality work experiences; in that case, there is pressure to provide the service to the team. An example is trending toward the gamification of learning solutions to adapt to generation Y/millennials' generation needs. Learning through gaming is one of the organizations' many issues in learning and development.

How do networked teams help with the development of leaders?

When learning as a team, the process becomes a little easier. A team understands that everyone learns differently, and it is in a smaller learning environment, so flexibility and adaptability are easier achieved. The natural diversity of the networked team also leads to a better learning environment.

Chapter 10

SCAN FOR VIRUSES

When studying the correlation between high-performing teams and effective leadership, one of the areas a researcher needs to explore is the issue that causes low performance and ineffective leadership. In a rich fertile entrepreneurial field in the United States, over 80 percent of businesses fail within the first seven years. In contrast, in the large organizational entities in Asia, you have organizations on life support and barely move year to year without reaching goals. What is the cause of these issues? It is the lack of awareness of what to do when there is low performance and inadequate leadership. Most leaders cannot correctly identify the issues in the team, which causes their ineffectiveness.

The objective of this chapter is to explore the challenges for leaders to learn to identify the causes of low team performance. I will call this a virus scan to keep up with our computer network analogy. All virus software starts with scanning the system. How does a leader properly scan for viruses in the team? After how, then what type of virus are they looking for? Virus software is limited to the code to train it what to search for, so the leader must understand what they are looking for in the team causing low performance.

How does the leader scan for viruses?

Teams are constantly influx in organizations. Often, it is because it is unclear what the organization gives the objectives, so it causes the team to suffer. The other primary reason is that inside the team, there are toxic levels of leadership that cause the team to perform at a low level. For this reason, a networked team learns to scan for the virus of toxic leadership to keep the team at a high-performance level. Most of us know the higher level of toxicity in leadership such as physical and verbal abuse. Still, more passive toxicity in teams comes from more passive behaviors.

Knowing What to Scan For

The prevalence of toxic leadership can harm a team through low performance due to the execution of tasks, effectiveness of decisions, communication with teammates and those the team service and the overall quality of work. The challenge is how a team can scan to understand if it is a virus causing the problem. Because of the lack of empirical research on the type of toxic leadership that destroys networked teams, some research findings allow the virus scan to be more effective.

A study showed that leaders act in destructive behavior 35–61 percent of the time, and the research of 2,400 workers in organizations showed that destructive behavior is not an anomaly. Among the respondents, 83 percent experienced some form of destructive behavior. The most destructive behavior experienced was laissez-faire leadership, accounting for 21.2 percent of the survey. The lowest was autocratic leadership at 3.5 percent. Even though this study shed light on the prevalence of destructive behavior, a valuable measurement tool was still needed for organizations to identify destructive behavior.

To reiterate, 21 percent of a toxic virus in a team is laissez-faire leadership. This means there are problems the networked teams need to solve that are overlooked for many reasons. Let's be honest—all teams will have some percentage of laissez-faire leadership, and we are not naïve to think the number would ever be 0 percent. Although there will be some passive toxic behaviors, the challenge is to lower that number to a level the team can tolerate and still perform well.

Measurement of Levels of Toxic Leadership

Often, toxic behavior is not adequately dealt with because there is no clear source to identify the virus. To help with the virus scan, we need to identify a tool to measure the toxicity of the virus. Shaw, Erickson, and Harvey (2011) created the destructive leadership questionnaire (DLQ) to assist organizations in identifying destructive behavior because destructive leadership can have harsh effects on productivity, revenue and profits, and team motivation.

Below is a list of toxic viruses that the team needs to scan. We are using an expansion of Einarsen's four behaviors and utilizing the eleven significant categories in the destructive leadership questionnaire (DLQ). The categories of toxic virus that leaders need to scan for are listed below.

Autocratic behavior

Why is acting in a noble or dignified behavior a toxic virus? Elitism or having a social order in a team is a toxic virus. This is especially true for networked global teams because you could easily create autocracy based on old colonial patterns. For this reason, a virus scan is done regularly to ensure there is zero autocratic behavior.

Poor communication

Poor communication is not just being able to form the proper sentences in an email or choosing a text to provide a detailed message that should have been done over the phone; it is a virus that causes toxicity in the team because the team sees the person as being rude, hurtful, or trying to exhibit that they are better than the others.

Unable to effectively deal with rogue team members

This laissez-faire behavior is a team virus that causes many problems. Rogue team members who are not adequately dealt with create a toxic environment that reduces the ability of the team to trust each other. Everyone makes mistakes, so the virus scan ensures the team owns up to mistakes and works to restore relationships. Rogue team members tend to keep creating conflict and friction because they cannot get over being wrong.

Poor ethics/integrity

Our most talented team members often believe they can lose their integrity because the team cannot function without them. This virus is usually combined with a rogue team member who is not dealt with properly. The lack of integrity in the team is a virus implosive to the team's system and processes. The scan of the virus is usually found when a teammate conveniently cuts down processes so they win and others lose.

Inability to use technology (also an overdependence on technology)

This virus scan needs to be more than basic Microsoft proficiency. The use of technology is understanding what/when/how the best for the team is. On the one hand, the team suffers if a team member doesn't know how to use technology and has either a lack of knowledge or overdependence. Technology usage is critical for networked teams, but we all need breaks, and the silent killer of networked teams is not disconnecting from the network to refresh and rebuild.

Inconsistent/erratic behavior

Yes, we love to laugh at shows like *The Office*, but it doesn't work for high-performing teams. Building a networked team requires consistency in actions and behaviors. The virus of erratic behavior is essential. Although everyone has a wrong moment, when there is a buildup of bad moments, the team suffers. The team has to scan for the virus by not allowing erratic behavior to continue without setting boundaries.

Poor interpersonal behavior

A networked team is a powerful tool for an organization. Even though you are not physically connected, you still have a powerful connection. Part of that connection depends on the ability to care for each other's needs. The virus of not caring for other teammates needs to be identified. A virus scan should show a team that has compassion for each other.

Micromanagement

The virus overcontrolling the team operations needs to be identified. Nothing slows a network faster than waiting for a team member to decide when the network should be free to operate. If decisions are slowed because of micromanagement, the team must scan for who is causing the slowdown.

Excessive political behavior

This could be just choosing a political party in today's environment, but this type of virus is different; it's the virus of constantly seeking power to get their way. Often, the teammate wanting to be right more than they want the team to succeed is evidence that this virus exists.

Lack of strategic skills

This virus is on the scan list because of the constant challenge to place the team in the best situation to succeed. The virus will keep the team from being in the right place at the right time. To compensate, each team member learns how to lead the team with a strategy. This is not just for one person on the team.

Update Your Software

How often has a teammate been excited about a new project, opportunity, or situation only to have a virus sneak in, and the excitement turns to apathy? Whether they are an employee, volunteers, or onlookers, the excitement is contagious, and after six months, the project, opportunity, or situation is no longer filled with excitement. Instead, it is filled with bitterness, anger, and vengeance. So what happened? Why was there a change in the team's perception of the situation?

The center of the problem is toxic leadership—not just the fact that there was a toxic leader but the team wasn't equipped with the skills to handle them. How do you, as a follower or a leader, respond to toxic leadership?

My goal is to outline a process to effectively communicate with toxic leaders and how to create an environment that produces a process to remove the toxicity caused by the destructive leader. The virus is not just about one person. Instead, it is about the team. A global leader in a networked team is to help one person while also keeping an eye on how to help the team. The process is based on the actions of the global leader when identifying the virus after a scan of their team then a process to help the infected and, finally, a process to help the entire team remove the virus.

What Do You Do When You Find the Virus?

A networked team has to keep virus software scanning for viruses regularly. A mistake we make during these situations is relying on the wrong perceptions which causes us to misidentify the virus. Most of the time, we base the label of toxic leadership on people we like or dislike. Whether a person is loud and obnoxious rather than quiet and not a bother to the group, the networked team must identify the same virus from a proper scan so there can be unity in removing the virus.

When I use the words remove the virus, many perceptions are wrong because we think we just kicked the person off the team, which is an oversimplification. It is important to understand that the primary goal is not to remove equipment from the network, which is a costly process and slows the networked team down considerably. The best solution is to handle the process of removing the virus with care and concern for the individual and the team, which is trickier and easier said than done.

Step 1: Isolate. How to help the infected

Once the infected teammate has been identified, isolate the person to help them recover from the virus in the network. Isolation is not a punishment but instead a time of reflection on issues. The time of isolation does not mean the person is on their own in finding solutions, but instead, they have a mentor or coach helping them remove the virus from their system. There are two primary ways this is accomplished. It is self-awareness and action planning.

Option 1: Help with self-awareness. A form of emotional intelligence is self-awareness. With self-awareness, a person has an intuition that something is not correct. Most of the time, the leaders will usually know when the team is operating effectively. So the team's leader has to decide: do they make the necessary changes to get the team on track, or do they allow the team to slowly die into a working group?

It is the same process for the individual who has been infected with the virus. They are exhibiting signs of infecting the team with the virus, and they do not want to be the person who slows the network so the team doesn't reach its objectives. They must be self-aware to sense that something is wrong with them. If the person gains this self-awareness, they are ready to move to the next step. If not, more isolation is required to bring them to that point. Removing from the team is the only option if they do not reach that point at a particular time.

Option 2: Action planning. The teammate has become aware of the virus they were carrying into the network but need a plan to remove the virus. Most of the time, the person will need an adviser, usually outside the team, to work with them in making the action plans.

Like most action plans, they need to be specific, which includes time periods and objectives. There is a strong sense of accountability in the team to build the trust level back. That is why the leader in the networked team is concerned not only for the individual but also for the team.

Step 2: Recode how to protect the uninfected.

Guilt and blame are two outcomes of a virus in a network that stops immediately. Before setting up a new strategy or a project that will resurrect the team, a leader takes care of the teammates impacted by the virus. A team must first heal, and the healing process starts with knowing they did nothing wrong to deserve the virus.

When a leader brings an infected teammate from isolation, they sense the hurt and should push forward to correct the team's path. Moving the team to effectiveness will often leave the relationship aspect out of the equation. In the meantime, there are people still hurting on the team. After isolation and when the networked team is brought back together, there is the next step of a recode. This is where relationships and processes must be recoded in the network to bring unity and get back on track for the team. The recode is what I term peace.

Describing and Defining Peace

The Greek word for peace is εἰρηνοποιός. This word means "to be at peace, live in peace, to make peace, be a peacemaker." Most of these phrases are active. So peacemaking is an active process, and leaders are the primary source of starting the act of bringing peace to their teams.

In leadership, we need to hear these words when we have pressures to make decisions during crises and conflicts. If the decisions made are wrong, the leader faces ridicule and shame. Other times, the decisions are correct, but the opposition is unhappy and hurtful things are said to and about the leader. Either way, there is a pain that comes with leadership. For this reason, there needs to be a proper definition of peace before describing how to gain this peace.

To start with a clear definition of peace, Merriam-Webster defines peace as "1. a state of tranquility or quiet: as a: freedom from civil disturbance b: a state of security or order within a community provided for by law or custom 2. freedom from disquieting or oppressive thoughts or emotions 3. harmony in personal relations." The word *harmony* is the usual definition as if you are a contestant in a beauty pageant, and a person says they want world peace.

Networked teams need peace after a virus infection is a harmony in personal relations. Since numerous issues arise during a virus scan and isolation, a networked team is tempted to worry or have anxiety during this crisis and conflict. In contrast, Strong's Greek lexicon defines peace (εἰρήνη) as "freedom from worry."

I have traveled the world serving global teams and heard stories of many challenges for their system and processes and personally experienced challenges in my leadership. During these times, the world seemed chaotic, harsh, and hurtful. I started to fixate on the concept of peace to break out of the bondage of worry, despair, and apathy. Can teams recover from a virus by being able to make peace? What does it mean for a networked team to have peace?

How do networked teams make peace?

If peace is available for leaders, why and how do leaders make peace? How does it affect those around them? After studying the concept of peace and learning about and teaching leadership, I have realized that peace is not an abstract idea. Still, it should be the focal point of those who desire to develop networked teams who follow their purpose through caring for each other, especially when returning from virus infection.

No one is exempt from the temptation of clicking a link to receive a virus, especially leaders in a team. As a team, we must be ready to forgive and make peace after the infected teammate returns from isolation. Making peace allows the network to push out the virus and return to high performance.

How does peace work in networked teams?

From my experience of working with global teams and seeing conflict within teams and organizations, and at times experiencing conflict in my teams and multinational business experience, a feeling of peace is needed to lower anxiety and increase harmony. Most teams do not want to operate in tension and conflict; they want harmony that allows freedom to operate without fear of attack. This harmony does not happen by itself. It takes the networked team to work in peace through authenticity, service, and doing the right thing.

Authenticity. Authenticity is a word used often in pop culture. There have been attempts to make authentic leadership a well-known leadership theory, but it did not have enough backing from research. This doesn't mean we cannot utilize this concept because I connect it with how the networked team uses genuine love through authenticity to reload the software after a virus infection.

A leader needs authenticity to impact followers, and in the case of crisis, the authentic or genuine action is to love the person or opponent. Genuine love is one filled with mercy and forgiveness. Genuine love is the first step to finding peace in a crisis like a virus infection. Without love, there is not much hope that you will make it through the crisis without anxiety, hurt, and pain.

Service. The following action is to serve. A networked team who serves each other in zeal provides a different perspective that allows for more effective ways of peace working in virus infection and reload of the team. The main reason is that a person passionate about serving will allow offenses to be forgiven. In other words, when experiencing conflict, a person serving with passion lets go and allows for resolution. During the reload, the work of peace shows that a person must not only love but also have a strong desire to serve others in the team and, in this process, seek a resolution.

Do the right thing. The final piece of peace in working in a networked team in a crisis of virus infection is to do the right thing. In this action, a person will not be self-serving but seek peace and do what is honorable. Doing the right thing is the key to overcoming a crisis of virus infection. If a team is grounded in doing the right thing, there is a high probability that the team will live at peace with all people because he will go the extra mile to solve conflicts with others. The person will take this action because they do not see themselves as better than anyone else.

Part 6

PRINCIPLE 5: COMPASSION

How a global team leader communicates with and treats the next generation of leaders is as important as the process. When working in networked global teams, leadership development is complex. Compassion is a complex trait to exhibit in one's culture and even more so in multiple cultures. Someone can easily fool you with their character and integrity by just knowing them from a few texts and seeing them on a flat screen. For this reason, the process shows many types of cognitive complexity when building nonlinear and unpredictable relationships.

To meet these complexities, the principle of compassion helps the team leader start a transformation process to lead the team's culture. The process of compassion then leads to the team's advantage in the success rate in learning and multiplication. The principle of compassion helps the globally networked team protect against viruses.

A networked global team learns the environment is always built about learning and growing, so compassion is critical to protecting the team from viruses. Part of the learning is how the teams multiply. The goal is not to grow bigger but to multiply and be more vigorous and build a better firewall against failure as a team for the organization.

Chapter 11

ANTIVIRUS PROTECTION

The salesperson usually asks if you want antivirus protection when you purchase a Windows computer. It is like they are saying that it is not if you will obtain a virus on your device but when you are infected with a virus, you need help. You need software that scans for you and isolates and removes the virus from the device. Notice that you do not go and purchase a new device unless it is rendered useless.

The challenge for networked teams is not trying to prevent a virus but for teams to be proactive in virus scanning and immediately respond to one if it appears. We discussed how to be reactive in the earlier chapters, but the following chapters will focus on being proactive.

Sometimes as leaders, we walk into a virus situation, and the first thought is that we need to do anything possible to remove the virus, and we do not think about the challenges our decisions will make in the long term. The challenge is with quick reactive decisions, and the virus is removed from one leader and given to another teammate. So the story repeats itself, and the networked teams feel like it deals with viruses more than focusing on achieving their goals and objectives.

Many leaders find themselves in teams with a virus and are only given short-term options instead of being proactive. The reactive mindset makes one feel like they are constantly tasked with resurrecting a lousy team.

Many times, global leaders are brought into a team, and they enter a situation and assess the problem and determine that the former team lost their way because the previous leader was not strong and exhibited laissez-faire leadership. So the immediate thought is to stop the virus and immediately push the team into hyper-productivity, and the new leader is overshadowing each step of the team. Another response from the new leader is to try to suck out the laissez-faire attitude in the team and replace it with tasks, high motivation, and diligence.

How do you think the team usually responds? At first, there is a short-term positive response, but eventually, a crisis or situation forces the team to rebel against the overly active new leader. The point is that most teams need to go from operating in laissez-faire mode and immediately turning on the task/motivation jets and becoming a productive team. An injection of antivirus software allows the team to make the changes necessary to become more effective.

What type of antivirus software is used for networked teams? That depends on the situation, but the new leader needs to use part of the venom to produce the anti-venom. For the sake of argument, I am recommending utilizing laissez-faire leadership. Still, it is constructed to allow the team to identify the venom and produce the antidote. Throughout this chapter, the task is to help with the process of identifying the antidote.

Create the Antivirus Protection

As I grow older, there are more opportunities for me to receive a shot, and I'm not too fond of needles, whether giving me a shot or drawing my blood. This fear does not just exist when I receive a shot but when I even watch others receive a shot. An example of this fear was the birth of my second daughter. My wife chose to deliver our first daughter without an epidural (shot in the back for pain). She was a little wiser in the second birth, so it was my first experience watching someone receive an epidural.

Many sitcoms or TV comedy is about the husband during delivery, and I could have been the central star. As the anesthesiologist uncovered the needle for the epidural, I immediately knew I was in trouble. It was such a big needle! Then I was to hold my wife as she was prompt to receive the shot. I knew I could not look, but to my horror and surprise, I could feel the pressure from the anesthesiologist inserting the needle. The nurse spotted my change of color, and I thought I would faint, so she quickly stepped into my place. It was a sharp pain for my wife when the shot was inserted, but it quickly removed the pain from the birth. As leaders, this is how we view the antivenom. The shot will initially hurt, but it will cure the problems of the organization and team.

The fear of needles is the same for many leaders when they find themselves in a situation where they have identified the bite and antidote, and now they have to inject the antivenom. A fear or phobia of the pain from a shot is the same as the leader has about injecting antivenom causing the leader to make the wrong decision. The leader is strong and sees the greater good of the organization when the antivenom is injected.

Injecting an epidural, the anesthesiologist has to know the small area in the spine. Just like the anesthesiologist, a leader has to know the exact location to install the antivirus software to not disrupt the normal operations of the networked team. It is an arduous process and not for the lighthearted. The leader understands their environment and situation and must be prepared for the initial pain caused by their decisions.

Up to now, I have been using this analogy of an installation of virus software, but leaders are not physically installing software into a networked team. So what practical ways are antivirus software injected in teams that know a virus is coming and want to be proactive? The following chapters will explore the process of running your antivirus software in your team. As I noted before, it often starts with sharp pain, but the goal is to relieve the more substantial pain caused by the virus.

There are three primary ways antivirus software is injected into a situation. The first step is self-learning. The second is creating diversity through the structure. The final part is adapting to one's identity.

Chapter 12

SELF-LEARNING

Creating an antivirus program requires the ability to learn; viruses adapt to their surroundings, so the program cannot be a one-stop shop. It can adapt to the team environment and make changes to prevent a virus from infecting the team. How does a networked team create this type of process? It starts with the ability to transform followed by being able to self-learn. When we combine these processes, it becomes transformation through self-learning. First, I will explain transformation and transformational leadership and, second, explain self-learning and development and, finally, how these processes help create the antivirus program.

Describing Transformation

Merriam-Webster defines transformation as a thorough or dramatic change in form, appearance, or character. The actual Greek word refers to metamorphosis: to be transfigured. A typical process is the metamorphosis of a caterpillar to a butterfly; the caterpillar goes into a cocoon and becomes a beautiful butterfly.

The process of metamorphosis is very similar to what happens during transformational leadership, the concept of which started in the 1970s. It is a landmark theory because it started a process that moved leadership studies from focusing on the leader to a focus on the follower.

In 1979, Burns wrote that leadership began the dialogue of transformational leadership as a theory. His definition was categorized into three areas, categories that were created to help describe the process of leadership when a leader inspires followers to accomplish goals or tasks beyond what they expect can be achieved.

I am using this description to provide the background for how transformational leadership helps create antiviral software. To show this process, we must connect the theory and process of transformational leadership with the self-learning system. I use Bass and Avolio's research into transformational leadership in organizations to accomplish this goal. They listed the four characteristics of a transformational leader titled the 4 I's.

1. The situation is ideal for influence because trust is involved. *Idealized influence* is an indicator of the number of trust followers have for their leader. The trust is built on respect, dedication, and appeal to their hopes and dreams. The leader acts as a role model, which adds to the desire for the follower to be transformed.

    Using the word *ideal* can be problematic in today's diverse environment. There are many issues surrounding a term like an ideal leader. Me, I would like to change this term to trustworthy influence. The word *trust* is easily understood across cultures. When you trust in someone, it comes with an act of following to meet goals and objectives.

2. *Inspirational motivation* measures how the leader inspires the followers through vision, organizational artifacts, and storytelling. The process produces a connection that makes the follower feel more significant in their work. Inspiration and motivation in one term are an interesting choice of words. Usually, to inspire is to motivate, but the goal is to show there is a feeling that leads to action.

    In the current environment, many organizations use the word *family* as a symbol to inspire people to join the organization. They tell stories of how a person joined the organization, felt like they were part of the family, and then achieved new heights in the organization. The outcome for the organization is that the follower is motivated to become loyal to the organization.

3. *Intellectual stimulation* encourages followers to transform old problems into new opportunities through creativity. This stimulation happens in an environment that welcomes ideas, even revolutionary ideas. The process causes an intellectual response that leads to the reflection of the follower's values and beliefs. The action is a more profound thought for the follower, stimulating others in the organization or team.

   When someone is working in a 2020 organization, intellectual stimulation comes from a form of pluralism. Processes, systems, values, and beliefs have a local context synchronized with the organization. Most of the time, the primary goal is for people to develop their ideas and creativity, creating new opportunities. Technology fuels the intellectual stimulation process, but it also can hamper the process. It is challenging to get to know each other virtually, and communication is usually formal, which takes out learning about the local beliefs and values.

4. *Individual consideration* is when the leaders show compassion and a desire to develop followers to reach abilities they never thought possible. For transformational leaders, this process doesn't happen in a group but individually. Not only is the individual relationship between leader and follower about their work performance but also it goes into their well-being.

   In today's organizations, the issue of mental health is critical. It is common to hear lectures on work/life balance. With many people transitioning to working from home, the balance has blurred even more. It is also more challenging to care for the follower's mental health. Regardless of where the person is, the leader finds a way to help a follower with individualized consideration. The action to help creates an environment to address mental health needs individually.

In all the descriptions of transformational leadership, there is a metamorphosis. The "caterpillar" leader only works through transactional leadership. Then this leader goes into a cocoon of development and explodes out of it as a transformed leader who inspires and is beautiful to their followers. We must first look at the caterpillar to learn more about this process.

The Butterfly

So the caterpillar turns into what? A butterfly is a beautiful creature, but its lifespan is limited. With the courage and endurance it takes to be a transformational leader, the process is best described in spurts. Burns describes transformational leadership saying, "Leaders and their followers raise one another to higher levels of morality and motivation." Do leaders switch between transactional and transformational leadership? There is a continuum for the global leader, which means the global leader will not always be in transformational mode, but they will live between the two.

Transformational leadership theory is a thought process that synthesizes theory and historical evidence of leadership with three primary concepts of transactional, transforming, and moral leadership with the end goal of developing a general theory that is now termed transformational leadership. Burns explores the concept of moral leadership by describing two main areas: purpose and power. The purpose is the crucible, and power is the fuel to go forward. Power is broken down into motive and resource. As a leader exerts relationships and gains followers, it is what the leader does with power that defines their morality. The essence of the leader and follower relationship is described as shared motives, values, and goals based on the followers' needs and those of the leaders who express, shape, and curb the conflict that comes from the needs.

To understand a networked team's transformational process, the first step is to describe the opposite: a transactional process. Bass says, "A leader is transactional when the follower is rewarded with a carrot for meeting agreements and standards or beaten with a stick for failing in what was supposed to be done." This type of transactional process is limited to a task manager position. The leader gives tasks that the follower completes, and then the follower is compensated. This process often happens in organizations but never works in a networked team.

A networked team process is more about influence and motivation. Bass explains that "transformational leaders motivate their followers to do more than the followers originally intended and thought possible." The team leaders set the goals and expectations for high achievement and then transform the team to reach those high objectives. When you read the explanations, which one do you want to be? It seems easy, but why do most leaders work with a transactional process?

Influential global team leaders desire their organization and teams to develop leaders that inspire and motivate followers to achieve higher goals than they ever thought possible. Achieving this goal allows for the type of antivirus software needed to keep the network at a high performance. This transition is crucial for global leaders and their ability to sacrifice for their followers.

Describing Self-learning

Once a transformation starts to happen in the globally networked team, the next step is creating a self-learning process so the team can use the transformation to learn how to keep future viruses away from the team. The challenge is not just selecting a development or self-learning process but creating a desire to learn about issues that directly impact the team's performance. To understand what this process would look like for a networked team, I will use examples using Boyatzis's theory of self-directed learning.

The core of the training is not in a classroom but focuses on the leader using self-leadership in learning emotionally intelligent characteristics. With three decades of experience developing leaders, Boyatzis created a developmental theory of five discoveries. With the five discoveries of my ideal self, my authentic self, my learning agenda, experimenting, and developing trusting relationships, the leader will gain more knowledge of their strengths and increase intelligence and emotional skills. The new knowledge and skills will increase motivation in specific roles.

The learning process is not sitting and listening to an expert teacher spewing information in loads; instead, it is based on experience and assessment. One way to categorize it is action learning. Action learning is a process that helps individuals and companies learn and develop as leaders while simultaneously solving problems through real-time solutions. Self-learning theory like Boyatzis increases the ability of action learning to help networked teams build an effective antivirus program.

Boyatzis's theory is based on trusting relationships that collaborate to support each other for each discovery step. This process aligns with the network team process and allows the team to help each other grow. The five discoveries are listed below.

My ideal self, whom I want to be? The leader helps teammates through individualized consideration (i.e., this is whom I want to be in the team to reach new heights as a group, starting with self-reflection).

My authentic self, who am I? (Strengths/Challenges and Gaps). The self-reflection leads to a reality check. We all have an ideal perspective of ourselves, but we need our team to help us see our strengths and challenges. The 360 view helps the growth of the team.

Learning agenda (Build on Strengths). Once the team helps each other with the reality check, you start the accountability process to build on strengths. We all have weaknesses, but many times, it is not worth the investment to make them better, but rather, continue to invest building on strengths.

Experiment and try new processes. The team also encourages accountability which is a new process of learning and growth. With the safety net of the team helping you grow your strengths, it is easy to experiment with new learning processes.

Developing collaborative and trusting relationships (Who can help me?). Since the team is working closely with each other, there will be a trustworthy influence that happens, and everyone on the team can help with learning and development.

There is no time to wait for a traditional learning process. Many organizations have implemented an action-learning environment in their training. Researchers use the terms *scientific* and *spontaneous concepts* to separate what is learned in a classroom and how a person learns in a social environment. Action learning and self-learning theories provide a collaborative, participant-centered environment that creates a learning environment with real-time solutions, which is critical for antivirus software.

The strength of scientific concepts lies in their conscious and deliberate character. Spontaneous concepts, on the contrary, are vital in what concerns the situational, empirical, and practical. These two conceptual systems, developing "from above" and "from below," reveal their real nature in the interrelations between actual development and the zone of proximal development (Vygotsky, 1986, p. 194).

Many challenges plague organizations in choosing the correct format for developing leaders. Most organizations will not care if a team uses the title *self-directed learning*. The focus is not on the title but instead on the outcome. The same question appears concerning the development of networked global teams. How can these leaders learn new leadership skills that will enhance their performance due to implementing the ideas directly into their role in the organization?

How Do Networked Teams Use Transformational Self-Learning to Create Antivirus Software?

The learning culture

Recently, I heard a commercial promoting the product's ability to detect malware before it enters the device. The detection process is based on artificial intelligence that adapts to the ever-changing threat of malware attacks. Artificial intelligence is based on understanding the team culture through the lens of transformational leadership developed through action learning from self and others. For networked teams, the transformational self-learning process is a type of program that can detect malware before it enters the network.

Basics of team culture

The global leader either develops a culture of fear (failure, loss, and conflict) or a culture of success (encouragement, inspiration, and fulfillment). The culture of success is what we term *transformational.* Team culture is an assessment of assumptions developed by a team as it learns to adapt to external and internal problems; the discussion and debate center on how the team culture adapts to challenges.

Leaders in the globally networked team have importance because their leadership is what forms, manage, and adapts the team culture. The transformation in the team culture compares what has worked well enough to be considered trustworthy, so these actions are taught to new members as the correct action. The challenge for team-networked leaders is distinguishing between local and global cultures while creating and managing the team culture.

How do global leaders impact the culture of networked teams?

The first challenge in transforming the networked team is perception. Miner says,

> The more favorable the perceptions of the potential follower toward a leader, the more the follower will model (a) the valences of the leader; (b) the expectations of the leader that effective performance will result in desired or undesired outcomes for the follower; (c) the emotional responses of the leader to work-related stimuli; and (d) the attitudes of the leader toward work and toward the organization.

How can a team transform when you are not meeting each other in person? Here "favorable perceptions" is defined as the perceptions of the leader as attractive, nurturing, successful, or competent. Of course, for the networked team, perceptions are based on communication through a screen or written text.

The second challenge is the process of leading and managing culture. As a global leader starts to influence their team, the need for transformation must be identified. The two primary transformation processes in the team culture are mechanistic and organic actions.

For mechanical actions, the outcomes are usually less satisfaction with employees, bureaucracy, and a constant set of rules, goals, and control measures. The actions are more transactional instead of transformational. This process often causes fear, loss, and conflict in the team.

The transformation of the networked team comes from organic actions. The organic process of impacting team culture often produces outcomes of higher quality climate and satisfaction with projects, innovation, creativity, support, and flexibility in the team. These outcomes are often associated with encouragement, inspiration, and fulfillment. To better explain, here is the list of the four I's of transformational leadership with organic actions in a networked team.

1. *Idealized influence* is when the networked team trusts each other through faith in their abilities and respects them individually. From this action, the organic process produces a team-building process that brings them closer together collectively, and they model organic actions together. It is a team process of building each other up to appeal to the team's hopes and dreams of high achievement.

2. *Inspirational motivation* is when a networked team shares a vision and uses symbols or images to keep the team focused on the challenges ahead. The organic process allows the team to be inspired by their work's significance while the symbols or images bring a camaraderie that keeps a close bond for the team. Many times, you will hear the team say they feel like family.

3. *Intellectual stimulation* is when the networked team bonds through the desire for high performance, and they encour-

age each other to reach their goals through high performance. The organic process allows a free space for radical ideas and positions and a nurturing environment that challenges the team's preconceived norms and individual culture. A networked team is where the mind feels safe to share ideas and creativity.

4. *Individual consideration* is when the networked team shows compassion, producing a caring atmosphere. It could be that a teammate is in personal danger with local issues, but the team takes care of them in unique ways. It could be family problems or anything that impacts their life and work. The organic process creates check-ins with individuals to listen to their cares and concerns. The networked team is so close as a team that they perceive issues before the person discusses the challenges in the team.

With the organic process, networked teams use the 4 I's to transform how the team operates to reach high performance. Although the 4 I's provide context, you still must have the ability to implement the organic actions, and that is where self-learning is essential. Below is an explanation of how the five discoveries from Boyatzis's theory help in the transformational process.

My ideal self, whom I want to be?

When looking at self-learning in a team environment, you must focus on more than just the individual. You connect it to the team and the organic process. The question of whom I want to be is focused on whom I want to be in the team. There are many choices, and people in a networked team can play similar roles, but the important part is that you are learning in the process. The process of idealized influence helps the person and team realize it is for the best of the team for everyone to realize their ideal self and grow toward that person.

Scenario. A team member is assigned as a lead to a project, but because they do not see themselves with the proper perspective, they become either laissez-faire or even apathetic in their leadership damaging the network.

My authentic self, who Am I? Strengths/challenges and gaps?

What changes do I need to make to be more natural and authentic? You must identify the gap when comparing your ideal self to your authentic self in a networked team. This allows the team to operate in a more organic way to inspire each other. Inspirational motivation helps the organic process by using symbols or images to promote growth and changes to help the team. Suppose a teammate acts in a way that is not their natural personality and ability. In that case, it causes problems identifying viruses because the team is surprised when they see the natural self.

Scenario. The team member identifies that they lack the confidence to lead the project and are causing virus-type issues for the network. The team member identifies growth areas for their engagement in the project to increase performance. The networked team comes together to inspire and motivate the team lead to make these changes.

Learning agenda—build on strengths, experiment, try new processes

Once a person on the networked team has the plan to bring them more to their natural or ideal self, they need to build on their strengths through the organic process of intellectual stimulation. Find creative processes that allow you to stretch and grow as an individual that will strengthen the team.

Scenario. The team leader for the project creates a plan to grow to the ideal self to block the virus of laissez-faire or apathetic leadership. The team works together to create a process that helps the project leader gain confidence and is much deeper than just confidence. It is setting up their ideal self to take on future projects that will be even more difficult.

Developing collaborative and trusting relationships—Who can help me?

Once you have experimented and developed a plan to grow as your ideal self, it takes the team to keep you accountable. With individualized consideration, the networked team feels like family and has a bond that produces accountability. This is not the legalistic type of accountability that is trying to point out what is wrong with a person but instead is a caring type of family member who is concerned about the well-being of the person and their growth into the ideal self.

Scenario. The care for the person and their growth is overwhelming. The trust and care inside the team are at their peak. Everyone feels significant in the process, and the team is reaching goals they never thought they would obtain because they are transformed as a team.

An antivirus is created from organic actions and self-learning that produces transformational networked teams. This is not just any antivirus but one that can adapt to malware before it infects the system. By combining the 4 I's and self-learning, a networked team is a solid force to fight off any virus that attacks.

Chapter 13

DIVERSITY

In the last chapter, I discussed the need for transformation through self-learning to create artificially intelligent antiviral software to keep the networked team working effectively and efficiently. In this chapter, I will discuss the need for diversity in a networked team and create the proper structure to build a firewall for the antivirus to protect the network.

Need for Diversity

In western culture, there is not a more discussed topic than diversity. Leaders in teams are asking if they have enough diversity? Does diversity matter even matter? Why do I feel pressured to be more diverse? These feelings come from the pressures of keeping within our boundaries. Our natural tendency is to gather in a community around people who look, think, and work like us. Is diversity always the answer? No, but when you build a networked team of diverse people who come together for a shared vision, it is more powerful than a team lacking diversity.

Gardenswartz, a researcher in the field of diversity, provides multiple dimensions of diversity. Understanding the dimensions and how a person identifies themselves is connected to how a leader will transform from a local to a global leader. For example, a leader in Cambodia will identify themselves according to age (older is better for leadership) and gender (males are more accepted in leadership). Their secondary identity will be education level, language (English efficiency), and family status. The organizational identity will be business, religion, and then location. The final identity dimension is cultural. At this point, the global leader develops an identity of "this is how my culture does it" to "this is how I adapt to other cultures by understanding how they do it."

The critical part of an emerging global leader is to identify as equal across cultures. Because the world of hegemonistic practices is still prevalent worldwide, a global leader must distinguish between people who see themselves as superior in cultures and races to build effective teams. Part of the debate and discussion in development is how to help global leaders identify in a way that increases their effectiveness as leaders to lead themselves, their teams, and the organization. The discussion starts with leader perceptions.

The influence of diversity on leadership practices

In the history of leadership perception theory, the first stage was developed in the 1950s which formed an implicit leadership theory. Historically, implicit leadership theory focused on leadership traits such as intelligence, dominance, sensitivity, strength, charisma, and tyranny. The social-cognitive revolution influenced research in the 1980s, and the focus of leader perceptions changed to perceiver expectations and biases. Research and assessments explored the follower's self-perceptions of leadership.

In the growth of global leadership, there is a push to understand leadership across cultures. Perceptions and effectiveness of leadership across cultures have led many researchers to suggest that leadership perceptions may not equate to global leadership effectiveness. A leader could achieve performance goals and not be perceived as effective by followers because of the emotions of perceptions. These emotions are often based on the local culture's perception of effective leadership.

One part of the research connected the processing of the sub-cortical structures to the perception of a leader. This is a critical part of understanding diversity in networked teams. Diversity is not about language and nationality, but differently, effective leadership is perceived; the networked team benefits from a diverse view of effective leadership. The question is, what constructs the diversity of leadership perspectives in a team?

The leadership categorization theory suggests that through socialization and past experiences with leaders, followers develop prototypes and subsequently use them during information processing. Leadership categorization was essentially pattern matching in which the follower matched the desired leader's traits and behaviors and matched the ideal prototype leader. In the perception of leadership, emotions, behavior, and matching were critical in deciding how followers rated the leader.

The challenge for a global leader in a networked team is distinguishing between perception and effectiveness from diverse backgrounds. For a networked team, the teammates will have different identity dimensions. Many team members would have a different perception of a leader and could underestimate their perceived effectiveness as the leader because of a different view of a leader. Westerners usually do not see leaders as strong when they appear passive and quiet like most Asian leaders.

In developing leadership in the team, the opportunity for growth is understanding feedback to understand the type of perceptions in the team. The networked team connects the local leader's identity to the global team's needs. From that point, you can connect the gaps for growth. The global leader must understand how their identity dimensions hinder their leadership and how identity dimensions impact how others perceive their leadership effectiveness. The complexity evaluating identity dimensions for a global leader is difficult.

Need for the Right Structure

A long list of books, articles, blogs, and podcasts spend a great deal of time discussing how to structure the team. As I have described earlier in the book, a networked team's structure is fluid and built around the demands of the team instead of one or two individuals in the team. The goal is to move away from roles and responsibilities and look more toward achieving the goal. This move will hopefully allow your team to gain a collaborative spirit and not one of the silos and independent processes. These are good general points, but what about the specifics in structure?

As members of the networked team develop and learn how to be effective, the influence spreads to people in their own culture and beyond. With this development comes a more significant challenge. The new challenge is deciding how to operate. Will their mode of leading include love, justice, and compassion, or to abuse power, control people, and desire honor? The discussion arises on how global leaders can ensure they develop in a way that contributes to the people in their influence. From research and practice, the global leader's effectiveness is found in the ability to serve.

The leadership theory of servant leadership is an emerging description of leadership. Greenleaf started the term in his seminal essay *The Servant as Leader.* Being a servant in the team aligns with the type of structure needed for the networked team to be successful.

In Greenleaf's essay, he defines servant leaders as

> a servant first… It begins with the natural feeling that one wants to serve, to serve first. Then conscious choice brings one to aspire to lead. The best test, and difficult to administer, is this: Do those served grow as persons? Do they, while being served, become healthier, wiser, freer, more autonomous, and more likely to become servants? And what is the effect on the least privileged in society? Will they benefit or at least not further be harmed?

With the underlying process built on Greenleaf's writing on the servant leader's motivation to serve, two concepts demonstrate how the servant leader is motivated to lead:

1. *Power and service.* The transition of the servant leader not only desiring to serve but also have the motivation to lead causes because the aspect of power is introduced. The area

of power and servant leadership causes many problems in creating a unified framework since theorists differ on the use and motivation for power. A desire for power can create a more effective leader, but the desire for power is focused on service. The servant leader can have power and motivation and continue to serve others.

2. *Power and motivation.* With empirical research detailing that cultures to differ in their expectations of power, titles, and organizations, the power distance for servant leaders is different. With servant leaders, there is a need for power, but the need is about a different way of handling power. For the servant leader, power is critical because of the need to serve. There is also a need for power in an organization to serve more people. How the servant leader manages the distribution of this power in the organization separates it from other theories.

As more organizations are expanding into multicultural settings, the demand for leadership is more than just on skills and behaviors. Still, the act of leadership focuses on how diverse backgrounds work together in teams; the ability to serve while managing power and motivation is performed through the leader's humility. In Jim Collins's best seller *Good to Great,* he labels a leader with humility as a "level 5" leader. To understand the art of humility in servant leadership, there needs to be a clear description of a humble leader and a practical framework of how humility impacts the networked team and provides accountability to team leaders when faced with power and motivation challenges.

Chapter 14

SENSEMAKING

Complex organizations have complex teams. Because of this, I suggest organizations use network teams to meet higher performance standards. When complex networks face crises and problems due to uncertainty, they gather information at a rapid pace. The problem with this process is that the information can cause an overload in the network. Too much information slows down the processes, and the networked team, which is supposed to manage complexity, is locked into a buffering process loop of information overload.

The way to prevent overload for the networked team is to have the ability to make sense of the situation to draw the information needed and not pile an enormous information dump onto the team. In the constantly connected world we live in today, this is very easy. The networked team must utilize the antivirus of sensemaking to prevent overload.

The primary area this virus attacks the networked team is during change events. Whenever organizations are faced with crisis events, whether from external or internal forces, the organization adapts to meet the challenges. In a networked team, adapting to external or internal forces should be a strength because a shared leadership model lends itself to adaptation. Even with this strength, a networked team can allow a virus because a strength becomes a weakness.

The networked team is too quick to adapt and needs to make sense of the changes; therefore, the change hurts the effort. To stop this from happening to the network, the antivirus software needs to prevent unnecessary change by understanding the adaptive challenge through making sense of the situation. Making sense is often connected to a sacrifice of local identity. To begin understanding the antivirus, a team leader must understand the concept of sensemaking and the need to meet adaptive challenges instead of just changing for change's sake.

The Concept of Sensemaking

Weick's seminal work on sensemaking helped organizations understand how to make sense of change. Sensemaking comes before decision-making. In the complexity of organizational change, there is chaos. A leader uses sensemaking to organize during the chaos. Inside the organizations, team leaders see the impact of proper sensemaking whenever the current state of the world is perceived to be different from the expected state of the world. Leaders organize through sensemaking by noticing and bracketing, labeling, retrospective, presumption, social and systematic teamwork, action, and organizing through communication.

Making common sense in communication

Communication is a crucial part of sensemaking for networked team leaders as a team leader's main activity is communicating the group's vision and goals to transform the group during change initiatives. The word *perception* is significant for common sense communication. The networked team perceives the communication of the team leader as credible and proven through credentials or experience, an extraordinary sense of purpose, and in the end, leadership is a difference maker in direction-giving.

The competency of sensemaking is critical for a networked team leader in strategic thinking to determine the need to adapt. The team leader can also make sense of the current situation and challenges, which is common sense. This means more people understand what the global leader is saying. When working in virtual teams and across cultures with different languages, common sense is crucial to describe this competency.

At first glance, the word *sensemaking* looks simplistic. It is a primary attempt to make sense of the context, surroundings, or environment. For global leaders, sensemaking seems simplistic but challenging in practice. Global leadership processes require sensemaking to be successful by utilizing the core elements of sensemaking. A networked team can prevent overload and make the right decisions on how and when to adapt to the complexities surrounding them.

Three Core Elements of Sensemaking

Research in sensemaking has identified three core elements for organizational and team leaders. They can explore a more comprehensive system outside the norms of decision-making, map the current system from reflection on problems, and change the system to learn more about the team. These three elements are critical for the networked team to utilize to prevent information overload.

Ability to explore

One of the areas in that networked teams and working groups are different is in the decision-making process. Working groups usually discuss potential options, but the final decision is usually just made by one person. In contrast, the networked team has a discussion, and any team member can decide. The decision is based on expertise in the area by that team member, and they provide the necessary information to the network.

The networked team often has multiple experts, so that is where information overload can happen. The antivirus option of sensemaking helps because of the core element of the ability to explore a broader system in decision-making. The other team members, although not experts in the area, provide accountability by providing a more comprehensive feedback system. The accountability is on deciding on time, with the correct information, and not a prolonged buffering of an overload of information.

Create a map of current systems

Like an architect who keeps blueprints of the building they created, a networked team keeps a map of the current systems. When a decision to adapt and change needs to be made, the team needs to know the map of current systems to decide rapidly and with adequate information. This is critical in stopping the virus of overload.

If a team must keep reviewing current systems and processes to remember how critical decisions are made, this causes the virus that slows down the team and their performance. A networked team has its map ready because they know the complexities of its work create constant chaos.

Change the system

The final part of the core elements of sensemaking is the ability to change the system to learn more about the team.

This could be moving a device to get a faster bandwidth for a network. Whether it works or not, the test needs to happen so you can make the network more robust. The networked team makes sense of adapting by not fearing moving the parts in the system to learn about the team.

How Do Leaders Make Sense of the Need to Adapt?

Once the networked team leader diagnoses the adaptive challenges, the need for change occurs; this is the critical part. The need for change only happens according to adaptive challenges and not because of trying to insert their agenda into the team.

Teams and organizations change rapidly, and global team leaders adapt. Even with the rapid pace, change is done in a process to stop viruses in the team or instead of helping, it breeds viruses.

As uncertainty around the world grows, challenges come from changes in natural circumstances, globalization, technology, and local governments. The ability to lead change in this environment is complex and takes a unique endurance that global leaders provide through understanding adaptive work. Networked team leaders can effectively communicate why change is needed, what needs to change, and how to change.

What adaptive change is needed?

The initial debate is understanding that change is a process/system. But with any complex system, there are many possible scenarios and outcomes. For a networked team leader, which process do they choose when challenged with adaptive issues?

Evolution or Revolution

Although organizational theorists agreed that change happened, there was much debate on how change occurred in organizations. Organizational change theorists distinguished change as episodic or continuous and revolutionary or emergent. Although there was a difference in the nature and process of change, a common theme about organizational change was that regardless of its origin, leadership is required.

Burke argued that integrating the study of management and leadership should increase the understanding and effectiveness of organizational change processes. To accomplish the integration, researchers needed to focus on various parts of organizational change and determine how each part affected and was affected during the change process. The challenge was determining the type of leadership that was the most effective during organizational change.

As in all research, there is another view of the process of the nature of change. Some researchers suggest that change is emergent, slow, and continuous. This process challenges the theory of revolutionary change by saying that to change an organization effectively, a leader focuses on the minor issues of change rather than the large ones.

Over the last year or so, we have seen that a global pandemic does not allow for evolutionary change. Many of us had to learn revolutionary change at a swift pace. Whether change happens evolutionary or revolutionary, the critical piece of the need for leadership is still the same. The team leaders must communicate clearly and concisely the roles of change, how resistance to change will be managed, and the commitment to change in the adapting process. This type of leadership is one that networked teams need to keep the virus of overload from entering the system.

Roles of Change

In the area of roles of change, there needs to be more clarity in delineating the words leaders and managers. A leader inspires others to act to understand why the team must adapt to the environment. Once the change strategy is created, then managers can define roles. Still, the leaders in the networked team keep a pulse on the process to ensure the roles do not become silos, leading to individual work, or even dismantling the team and making it a working group.

To keep the networked team from following the rigid role process of a traditional change process, I will utilize Conner's role strategy for change. Conner shows more of a triangulation of these roles comprised of sponsors, those with the power to enact change; agents, the ones responsible for the change; and targets, the individual or groups that must change. By Conner's definition alone, there is an excellent example of leaders (sponsors), agents (managers), and targets (followers).

In the organization, the networked team is the sponsor of change. Because of their ability to adapt and provide expertise for the project, the networked team has the skills necessary to lead the change process for the organization. Therefore, it is essential that the networked team does not have the virus of overload and makes sense of their role as sponsors.

The networked team plays the primary role in the change process as the sponsor. Specifically, the sponsors are a team in the organization with the legitimate power to make the changes. To understand why a networked team cannot allow for the virus of overload, the following are five primary characteristics that the networked team keeps from allowing an overload.

1. Power is critical in the change process. Who creates, implements, and manages the change strategy is responsible for the success and failures of the process. Communication cannot be an overload of information. It must be clear and concise to inspire others to act.

2. Most of the time, change happens because of a problem that is causing the team and organization pain. A networked team as a sponsor should be able to use sensemaking to think outside the normal change process to make critical decisions. The sponsor feels the pain like the followers, and using the compassion part of a networked team should be their strength.

3. Vision accomplishes the change process that shows the followers where the organization is going. Their vision is to continue growing the team and organization.

4. Monitoring plans is not micromanaging; they are engaged in the process. The sponsors make sure they stay apprised of the developments of the organization.

5. A willingness to sacrifice for the vision is what followers want to see in their sponsors. Will the sponsors sacrifice for the vision? Will they make the decisions that will take endurance to enact?

Resistance to Change

When leaders encounter resistance to change, they usually fail to evaluate. Evaluating the change process was rare for organizations because leaders do not usually push through challenges and barriers. The networked team is different because they use their ability for sensemaking to evaluate not only what is good about the change initiative but why and how they are leading through resistance. Make no mistakes, leaders, there will always be resistance to adaptive work.

Evaluation helps organizations understand what worked and what didn't during change implementation. The virus of overload could convolute the evaluation process. For this reason, the networked team needs to understand what specifically to evaluate.

What to evaluate during the adaptive work and change is the final piece to stop the virus of overload; the following are examples:

1. Denial is when the team and organization cannot process new information for change in their current system.
2. Anger is demonstrated when there is high frustration, and the response to the communication is irrationally lashing out at the networked team.
3. Depression is a normal response to negatively perceived change. The team exhibits acceptance of failure and a lack of emotional and physical energy, and disengagement or quiet quitting are forms of team depression. An outside environment, such as a global pandemic, can also influence depression in the team.

Commitment to Change

As the networked team understands their role as a sponsor and learn to evaluate resistance to change, the next step is to commit to change. The word for a commitment to change is *resilience*. It takes dedicated leaders who will endure resistance for the greater good of the team and organization. In building resilience, one of the main factors for leaders is to show their ability to commit to the changes they sponsor. Commitment is another complex issue that requires multiple stages during the change process.

The three stages of resiliency in commitment to change are preparation, understanding, and the ability to install. These stages are centered on the leader's self-awareness, listening ability, and strategy implementation.

Preparation

The first stage of commitment. In this stage, there are two immediate actions for the leader. They are contact and awareness with targets. Contact is done through meetings, speeches, and other forms of communication, but they only sometimes build awareness. The action of awareness is when the leader knows the modifications discussed during the contact phase are in process.

Understanding

To understand means the leader must know how the team learns. In his classic work on change, Schein shows that knowing how the team and people impacted by the change strategy understands is a significant piece to success in the change process. With the team leaders communicating effectively through contact and awareness, those in the change process are aware of and comprehend the change and can now make sense of the situation.

Ability to implement

As networked team leaders start to experiment and test the change initiative, there must be an ability to turn ideas into action. In this process, the leader encourages open discussion with the team to gain positive and negative feedback.

Part 7

THE EXAMPLE

When reading the New Testament, we probably don't think it could teach us how to lead virtual teams. As we look closer at the ministry of Paul, we see evidence that he not only created but also led virtual teams to provide the structure needed to grow a global church. As we look back to his accomplishments as a global Christian leader, we are amazed at his success in launching churches throughout Asia and Europe. How did he accomplish this global leadership process?

Creating and leading high-performing global teams is hard in the current environment with our technology and fast travel. How did Paul accomplish this feat with letters that took months to arrive and not knowing what the team was doing on a day-to-day basis? Reading the book of Acts, we know he created real teams, not working groups. Below is a table with his virtual team's position/role, mission, and location.

Chapter 15

CASE STUDY

Paul's Global Team

Name	Position/Role	Mission	Location
Apollos	Evangelist	Preach/teacher	As needed
Barnabas	Travel team	Global church governance	As needed
Epaphras	Evangelist	Plant local churches	Colossae
Aquila/Priscilla	Leadership development	Grow global churches	As needed
Hymenaeus	Teacher, leadership	Plant churches	Ephesus
James (Jerusalem Council)	Board/Elder	Global church governance	Jerusalem
Lydia	Administration/ finance	Sustain the local church	Philippi
Mark (Barnabas's nephew)	Administration	Serve in the global church	Ephesus
Onesiphorus	Team player	Serve Paul	Rome, Ephesus
Onesimus	Messenger	Serve the global church	Rome, Colossae
Philemon	Elder	Leader/Elder/ Provider of the local church	Colossae

Phoebe	Deaconess	Serve the local church	Concrete
Silas (Silvanus)	Travel team	Mission strategy	As needed
Timothy	Travel team	Mission strategy	As needed
Titus	Travel team	Mission strategy	As needed

You identify three areas of expertise when you assess Paul's movements, decisions, and testimony. These three areas helped Paul achieve this goal of planting churches throughout Asia and Europe. They are the following:

1. Strategic expansion

    Paul had a clear mission to preach the gospel to the unreached. Each team member was part of this mission, and he utilized their abilities to help accomplish the calling he had from God. He even had a place he wanted to reach: Spain.

2. Agile governance

    In a working group, the leader creates a hierarchal structure that depends on the top leader to make all decisions. Although Paul was influential in the decisions, he created teams because of their strategy to plant churches among the Gentiles. The teams could not depend on a strict structure but needed the ability to be creative and serve the local churches in a context that would work in their situation.

3. Leadership development

    Paul knew he could only have a long-term impact on these regions if he developed leaders. There were two areas he needed to develop leaders: global leaders on his team and local leaders on the ground who would provide stability. How did he accomplish developing leaders in an environment where he did not stay for a long term?

What about Today?

Things have changed some since Paul walked the earth. As we have shown, a networked team is not about technology, but technology does help, and clear communication is also important but not the answer. The networked team needs strategic expansion, agile governance, and leadership development to succeed with or without technology.

Below is a COVID era case study to help understand how the networked team works in the current environment. The key to understanding is not whether you have the technology but whether you are a team leader. Leadership in a team surpasses all things. You can have the best product, technology, or systems, but you need team leadership to be valid.

Modern example

In 2018, a global consultant was approached by an organization that wanted to expand to regions around the world. The goal of the expansion was to develop a global/local strategy. The global platform would allow the user to gain an incredible experience, but the local process would provide a more profound learning process. Below is a table that describes the design of the networked global team. The results are still in process, but the fact that it has grown to these regions during a global pandemic and recession shows that the network is sustaining the processes.

The Networked Global Team Design

Global Team	Strategic Expansion Challenge: Localized product with global platform.	Agile Governance Strategic expansion through teams.	Leadership Development Talent acquisition and development
Latin America	19 Spanish-speaking countries in LATAM.	A large hub pushing strategy with HQ support but not control.	A formal process with HR director hiring top global talent.
South Asia	India alone accounts for 100s of languages. Which language is localized?	A medium hub learning from other teams and using HQ more as partner than support.	A networked process with hiring only within their past network.
UK	Localized product without a large presence of US thought leaders.	A small but knowledgeable hub with freedom in decisions while connected to HQ for services.	The team was formed previously and moved over to this project.
Brazil	Who is the local partner to champion the product?	A smaller hub that has a stronger network with partners.	Still working on formation, finding some roles but mainly a small network working closely together.
East Asia	Localized product exceeds performance of global platform.	A medium hub that is a mixture of on-the-ground and partnering process.	A formal network with process and systems in place.

West/Central Africa	Multiple tribal areas expanding across borders. Which language/ custom is first to be localized?	A small hub that struggled to find the right mixture of the network.	Informal network with a high control from one leader causing slower development.

To achieve this goal, there is a need to create teams across regions that could implement the global/local strategy.

Strategic expansion

The organization has a clear mission and vision, but how does it translate across cultures? As the organization was choosing to expand, there were many challenges, including which regions had a higher probability of purchasing the service. What regions could localize the product? Which regions had the talent to lead local teams?

Once these questions were answered, then the selection of the team started. The directors would directly report to the international team at HQ, but the director would have autonomy in building their team. These regions would create teams that would be networked to headquarters but not directly, and they would be connected through the director who would act as a hub.

Agile governance

It became apparent during the setup of the strategic expansion that there would not be the ability to govern the regional teams through headquarters. The contracts provided some governance but only for the more significant issues. Day-to-day operations had to be agile because we were learning the processes and procedures in a new market.

Leadership development

When a company is expanding globally with a new product offering for most people around the world they desire to serve, there is a proven leadership development process. When people see the word proven, they think of a class or group of lessons, but for an environment such as entering global markets during a global pandemic, there was no option for a formal program. It had to be done with agility, empowerment, and trust. The release of control to allow leaders to develop was critical to the strategy's success.

Chapter 16

FALLING FORWARD

My goal with this book was to provide you with the concepts and ideas to create, design, and operate a networked global team because the opportunities for those teams are tremendous. The global projects that impact our world in an excellent way need a concept of teamwork that transcends the process of a team sitting face-to-face at the headquarters. Networked global teams provide the ability to meet the needs of global organizations.

I often end a workshop with the encouragement of falling forward. The reason is that there is a growth curve whenever leaders embark on new systems and processes in global leadership. It will feel like you are falling with the pressures that mount during the adventure. The goal is that you fall forward to show growth at each step of the way.

To end the book, I want to provide you with five ways to fall forward as you start the venture of either starting or improving your globally networked teams. This helps you think and reflect on your global leadership and develops a growth process for you and your team. The five processes are not linear or step-by-step approaches to creating or improving your networked global team, more like a description that allow you to use them wherever you are creating the team.

Show urgency but be kind, patient, and just. When a leader starts the change process, they must show a sense of urgency so others will sense there is a need to change. Often, this sense of urgency causes conflict and general uneasiness in the team. This is not bad, but you must make sure to be kind to one another during the conflict. Next is to be patient when others do not have the same sense of urgency. The final part is to be just when deciding how to hold the team accountable to the urgency.

Show compassion by desiring to teach others. A leader with compassion is one to behold. Followers need and enjoy a compassionate leader, especially one that uses compassion to have the desire to teach others. The networked team process takes time to learn, and often, team members will gravitate to the old ways in which they are more comfortable (even though they admit they are less efficient). To keep the team on track with creating and designing a networked team, a leader is compassionate for their team, and this compassion is exhibited through a desire to teach. A leader cannot leave the team alone to figure it out independently; there is a learning and growth part of the process.

Think deeper by taking the time to reflect on good and bad. Most leaders are so busy that it is difficult to stop and think. For this reason, they usually stay at a surface level, and more profound thought is never realized. When designing and creating networked teams, the leader cannot stay in a state of surfaced thinking. It takes a more profound thinker as a leader not just to contemplate the bad but also to understand the good in the process.

Test ideas regularly because you cannot give up on the process. The creation or transition to a networked global team will take the ability to experiment with your ideas. These ideas come from deeper reflection; even though they are good in your head, they still need to be tested in the real world. The problem with any test is that sometimes it does not work the way you want, which can be discouraging. From the discouragement, there will be a temptation to stop the tests, but this would be a mistake. You test to find the best fit for the network regarding talent, placement, and building, so even when you are discouraged, you cannot give up on the process.

Enjoy the moments when it shows progress. It would be best if you enjoyed those moments as a team when you succeeded in the process.

Do not allow them to slip by and start on the next step. In the act of enjoying the moment, there are also teaching opportunities because we tend to reflect more when we are relaxed and joyful. Also, with the urgency and intensity of creating, designing, and implementing networked global teams, everyone needs to relax and have a good time.

Conclusion

The steps described above are the fall forward for you and your team. As always, in leadership, it is never a transparent process to growth. Leadership development is a messy, nonlinear process that takes the ability to take one step back so you can gain two steps.

Creating, designing, and implementing networked global teams is also messy. If you follow these steps, it will be a success, but there are too many variants to provide you with that perfect prescription. What I do believe is that we need help in this global environment. We cannot do it alone, and that is not just individually but our own culture. A networked global team is the best organizational growth and development option.

About the Author

Jay is dedicated to practicing, researching, and teaching global leadership for over two decades. His practice of global leadership started when he gained valuable insights on strategy development, management challenges and practices, and leadership development.

From his experiences of working in emerging markets around the world, Jay developed the Nextgen Global Leaders Program—a program for corporations and nonprofit organizations that are transforming into global companies and need to identify, train, and manage top talents to expand globally. To expand the NGLN, Jay founded Nextgen Global Leaders in Singapore in 2015 to serve Asian organizations in developing global leaders, followed by organizations in the Middle East and the United States.

He utilized his research in global leadership and teams to publish his first book, *The Five Principles of Global Leadership*. Jay earned a PhD in leadership studies from Carolina University, a master's in business administration from Auburn University, and a bachelor of science in management from the University of Alabama at Birmingham.